IRON MAIDEN & PRAYING MANTIS
The Early Days

Bob 'Angelo' Sawyer

IRON MAIDEN & PRAYING MANTIS
The Early Days

Bob 'Angelo' Sawyer

WYMER PUBLISHING
Bedford, England

First published in Great Britain in 2018
by Wymer Publishing
Bedford, England
www.wymerpublishing.co.uk
Tel: 01234 326691
Wymer Publishing is a trading name of Wymer (UK) Ltd

Copyright © Bob Sawyer / Wymer Publishing.

ISBN 978-1-908724-84-7

Edited by Jerry Bloom.

The Author hereby asserts his rights to be identified
as the author of this work in accordance with sections
77 to 78 of the Copyright, Designs & Patents Act 1988.

All rights reserved. No part of this publication may be
reproduced or transmitted in any form or by any means,
electronic or mechanical, including photocopying, or any
information storage and retrieval system, without written
permission from the publisher.

This publication is sold subject to the condition that it shall not,
by way of trade or otherwise, be lent, re-sold, hired out or
otherwise circulated without the publishers prior consent in any
form of binding or cover other than that in which it is published
and without a similar condition including this condition
being imposed on the subsequent purchaser.

Every effort has been made to trace the copyright holders of the
photographs in this book but some were unreachable. We would
be grateful if the photographers concerned would contact us.

Typeset by The Andys
Printed and bound in Great Britain by
CMP, Dorset, England

A catalogue record for this book is available from the British Library.

Cover design by The Andys.
Cover photos © Bob Sawyer.

CONTENTS

BEGINNINGS	1
PRE-MAIDEN	7
IRON MAIDEN AND ME	15
FOR IRON MAIDEN TRAIN SPOTTERS: EQUIPMENT LIST	31
IRON MAIDEN'S GIGS	33
ON THE ROAD WITH PRAYING MANTIS	39
PRAYING MANTIS: BETWEEN THE TOURS	59
THE PROFESSIONALS GET HOLD OF US!	71
THE MAJOR OFFENSIVE: MAIDEN'S FIRST BIG TOUR	75
THE AFTERMATH — A BOLT FROM THE BLUE	127
POINTS OF TRIVIA	133
GUITAR TRIVIA	135
WHERE ARE THEY NOW?	137
OTHER ENCOUNTERS	140
ACKNOWLEDGEMENTS	144

BEGINNINGS

I come from Enfield, a suburb of North London, the only Son of Ron, a design Draughtsman (he designed the machine that wraps 'Rizzla' cigarette papers) and Joan, who was a company cashier. My father fought in WW2 in Burma... he fought the Japanese at the famous Battle of the Irawady River (at the tender age of 19). The area I lived in until my early twenties was called Ponders End. The only other 'celebrities' that come from my area are, Dave Peacock, of Chas and Dave and actress Jessie Wallace, of *Eastenders* fame... she lived down my road, and I actually worked with her father, as a telephone engineer, in the mid seventies.

As a kid, I was smitten by the sound of the electric guitar. When I was nine my mum bought us a record player and the first 45 rpm single she bought me was 'I'm a Moody Guy', by Shane Fenton, which I still have... and reckon is one of the best early sixties British rock 'n' roll records, better than anything Cliff and The Shadows ever did!

I became totally besotted with The Shadows and the American guitarist Duane Eddy. When I was ten my parents bought me a cheap Spanish guitar. It was so hard to play, that I nearly gave up but I just had to learn to play, like my heroes. I lapped up their records, which were mainly bought for me from the market stall in Enfield Town, or at Hatch Brothers, an electrical shop in Ponders End that sold records as a sideline. I nearly died and went to heaven, when I found out that Duane Eddy and I had the same birthday! (April 26th). I had the great fortune to see Duane Eddy live, at the Regal Cinema Edmonton in November 1963, on a package tour, which included Mickie Most (before he became a top record producer) and various others, including Little Richard... whose act was outrageous! At the climax of his show he threw his shirt into the audience, who fought over it like wild animals, eventually tearing it to shreds. Jesus Christ! I thought I have just got to have some of this!

With my cheap Spanish guitar, I started to learn to play... Shadows, Duane Eddy and anything guitar oriented, and at the age of 13, I bought a Hofner Senator guitar and a Selmer Little Giant amp ,which is hardly a rock 'n' roll combination made in heaven (both are worth a small fortune nowadays) but to me it was a step in the right direction.

In September 1963, I started at the Ambrose Fleming grammar school in Enfield, and at Christmas 1963, they had a Christmas concert. To my utter amazement all these nerdy kids came on stage playing electric guitars, all Hofners, Burns and Watkins Rapiers etc, through tiny little 15-watt amps. This must have been (alongside the Duane Eddy and Little Richard gig), my biggest inspiration to form a group and the next year at Christmas... it was our turn. We were called The Silent Flights with me on harmonica, (for some unknown reason, I didn't play guitar) Dick Stringer on guitar and John Kitch (my lifelong friend and drummer in Nitro Blues in the 80s) on vocals and maracas. We were 'amateur' to say the least, but it got the ball rolling. The three of us later formed The Younger Set, which included Alan Ross on guitar and vocals. Ross later released loads of albums with his own band in the seventies and he also played acoustic guitar on The Who's *Tommy* soundtrack.

I played in many local bands in the late sixties and early seventies, including Purple Impact, Under Negotiation, Big Ladder Woman, Moby Dick and Stone Kerb... playing in youth clubs, dance halls and discos, and never made any money, all of it going on HP charges for guitars, amps and PAs and on dodgy vans and other expenses, but none of us really thought about the money side of things, it was all great fun.

In Enfield in the mid sixties there was quite a good local music scene, mainly centred around youth clubs and local dance halls, and there were a lot of local gangs who used to come to gigs ... just to fight... or at the very least beat up the bands (or 'groups' as they were still called in those days). I personally didn't get harassed, as I knew a lot of the local 'hard cases', but I have seen some terrible carnage at local gigs. On one such occasion was at the Kingsmead School Dance in Enfield, back in March 1968. Whilst I was playing in the band Under Negotiation, we were playing our spot when "The Brimsdown Mob" decided to pick on a few peace-loving locals. Before long, the hall had erupted into what looked like a medieval battle right before our very eyes. By the end of the evening the whole school was wrecked... and the top band that night, The Stack had all their gear and their beloved 'ambulance', totally wrecked. The girl who organised it (Susan McGuire) had to face the headmaster on Monday morning with a lot of explaining to do.

All the local bands... that is The CBU, The Yes & No, The Harp, P T & The Clubman, The Mixed Bag and the top band, The Stack used to drive round in little beaten up old vans — Bedford Dormobiles; Thames 15cwts and Commers. But The Stack had an old ambulance. I remember it always breaking down and the back doors were always falling off!

The great revolution in group transport came along in August 1965, when The Ford Transit was introduced, the small 15 cwt version cost about £865 and the monster version... a six wheel 35cwt Goliath, that by the early seventies had become the benchmark for group transport, was over £1100 — an absolute fortune in those days!

Apart from London's Denmark Street in W1 where all the guitar shops were (sadly, there are very few left) the only local shop for guitars and amps, was Berry's, at the Angel, Edmonton. The shop was about two minutes walk from the Regal Cinema, where I had seen Duane Eddy and Little Richard. My first amp, which, as mentioned, was a Selmer Little Giant had an output of 4watts. Only really a bedroom practice amp, which I dutifully brought brand new from Berry's in summer 1965 for 12 guineas, which was all my pocket money that I had saved up for years. I still have that very amp, and it is part of my collection of vintage Selmer's that I have had featured in collector's books and magazines, for they are extremely rare and sought after nowadays.

I can remember the first time I played my Hofner through an amp with John Kitch, around at his place. He lived above his dad's fruit and veg shop in Enfield Highway, where he had a playroom in the converted loft. Kitch was an electronic buff as a teenager and he built a 10-watt amp with the speaker mounted on a separate board. When he finally got this amp to work, we plugged in my Hofner... turned it up full and I hit an E chord. I can still remember the excitement that I felt. I just had to get my very own amp, hence the purchase of the 'Little Giant'. My mum and dad were bemused by my interest in groups and beat music but dad was concerned that it would draw my attention from my schoolwork... and he was dead right! Throughout my teens, I was only interested in guitars, amps and girls. Needless to say I only got two GSE 'O' Levels... because I couldn't focus on anything academic (and I still can't).

After the Younger Set had run its course, the next band I joined was the Purple Impact. Aside form myself on guitar there was, Pete 'Pierre' Sturgeon on drums, Clive Barker on bass and Dave Andrews on vocals. This lasted throughout that incredible summer of 1967, until I got 'head hunted' (blimey!) by Under Negotiation, a band consisting of local hard cases; 'Milky' Smart on vocals, Kelvin Hardman (yep... his real name) on bass, Doug Webb on lead guitar and 'Twinkle' Boreham on drums. They even had (hard case) roadies! The first casualty was poor old 'Twinkle' His drumming was err... shite. So, at my suggestion, we brought in 'Pierre' Sturgeon.

We played all the local youth clubs and dance halls, gigging furiously, until I discovered the 'blues' and got seriously into stuff like Cream, John Mayall, Chicken Shack, etc, and thought... 'I can't be playing this pop shit anymore...' and gave in my notice.

After I left Under Negotiation in April 1968, I didn't play in a band for two years (through sheer laziness) and I consider that to be the biggest musical mistake I have ever made. By the summer of 1970, I was back in a band with my old school mate 'Pierre' Sturgeon. We were called Johnny and the Gumboils (it beggars belief, doesn't it?) It was a 'free form' band of passing hippies... all very 'improvisational'. After all, this was 1970.

The band started of as a six-piece, but by late 1970, it had evolved into... Big Ladder Woman, a power trio, where I was singing and playing lead guitar. That lasted until late 1973, before everyone lost interest.

Above:
November 1970 supporting Hawkwind.
Below:
Big Ladder Woman, May '72. L-R: Mick Sherman, me & 'Pierre' Sturgeon. Pierre's father was chauffer to the famous WW2 General Montgomery, no less.

The original bass player with Big Ladder Woman was Chris Gunnell, nephew of the legendary Rick Gunnell, a big rock promoter in the sixties (John Mayall, Georgie Fame, Yardbirds, etc.) After him came the infamous 'Spider Clarke', a thug dressed like a Hippy, a pretty odious character and general 'nasty bastard'... but he was very amusing, and you couldn't help liking him!

The next bass player (as you can tell, they seem to be a weak link in this band) was Peter Barnes, who lasted from January - May '72. He was replaced by Mick 'the wick' Sherman.

After that came Moby Dick, Stone Kerb, Nitro and Snatch.

Above:
With Big Ladder Woman, October 1972.
Right:
Big Ladder Woman
at the Sundown, July 1973.

PRE-MAIDEN

The story really starts summer 1974 when I went for an audition at the Alan Gordon Studios, Leytonstone, for Tiger Lilly, a band that contained Chris Aylmer (who later went onto Samson), Vic Scott, and Dennis Roy Willcock. At the audition they had me playing 'Rocky Mountain Way' and Mott the Hoople's 'Thunderbuck Ram'. I had to leave early due to an urgent phone call, which miffed them and I never heard from them again.

Over a year later, in September 1975, Kevin O'Brien and I had a trio called Nitro. We decided we needed a singer, so we put an ad in The Melody Maker as all bands did in those days. We auditioned a cast of idiots, one of which I must tell about. He had (starting from the head) a big white 'Rubettes' cap, a brown sequinned jacket, flares halfway up his legs and what looked like builders wellies with platforms! As if his image wasn't bad enough, he opened his gob to sing and sounded like a newspaper seller! Kevin and I were biting our lips trying not to laugh, but we just stopped playing... both sobbing and giggling! This poor bugger knew what was going on, and he was as red as a beetroot with embarrassment! He just said "sorry I wasted your time" and left immediately. We could barely manage a "thanks for coming", as we were still in tears of laughter.

The next 'contestant' walked in, larger than life itself, sporting a big Ian Hunter/Roger Daltrey 'barnet'. It was a second encounter with Dennis Roy Willcock. He was light years ahead of all the other 'contestants', so I offered him the job on the spot, after he had sung a few rock standards. I later discovered this miffed Kevin and our drummer Glenn, because I didn't consult them. I can be a bit impetuous sometimes.

He hadn't been in the band for long before things started to go a little err... sour. He engineered Glenn's demise and got in Vic Scott from Tiger Lilly who turned out to be a fucking nutter!

The next move was to get another guitarist, I don't quite remember whose idea that was, but we took on Alan Warner who had been in The Foundations back in the late sixties and had had a big hit with 'Baby Now That I Have Found You'.

Just before Alan and Vic joined we were gigging at The Cock pub, Edmonton one night and Kevin and I tuned up together but not necessarily to standard pitch, as electronic tuners were a long way off from being invented. Half way through the set, we launched into The Stones 'Midnight Rambler' and so Dennis grabbed his 'gob iron' and started wailing. But because we weren't in standard pitch, the harmonica sounded agonising. Poor old Dennis was doing his best to bend the notes but to no avail. Once again, Kevin and I were in tears of laughter... and so were most of the audience! I can still see that look of terror in Dennis's eyes as he struggled hopelessly to make the harmonica sound tuneful. I don't ever remember us playing that song again!

Things weren't going right with the band... plots were being hatched and I even found myself on the 'outside' of my own group, a situation which I really didn't like. After Christmas 1975 I decided it was time to look elsewhere. In the first edition of Melody Maker of January '76, there was a box ad saying: "Band Seeks Guitarist with Kossoff/ZZ Top feel". I couldn't ring the number fast enough.

I spoke to a certain Danny Hynes on the phone and a meeting was called for

that Thursday evening at their manager's place in Chiswick. On meeting the band we all got on very well and I had Danny in stitches of laughter with a string of (what is now very unpc) Irish jokes. He is from Dublin with a great sense of humour.

I auditioned with Snatch at the old Sound Management studios in Kings Road, Chelsea. At one point during the auditions, I was face to face... duelling it out with ex-Silverhead guitarist Steve Forrest, but I got the job and believe me, was in absolute heaven! The band had everything that you could possibly want, image, management, a 1000 watt PA and a three ton truck, what more could I ask for? A bit more Snatch trivia... guitarist Brian James (who later formed The Damned) also went for the guitar job with Snatch.

I loved being in Snatch but we only managed about three gigs before it ran out of steam. I can't quite remember why, but I had left my job as a GPO Engineer (after eight years) to "turn pro", so I had to do something. I was soon offered a job in a show band on their way to Germany with 'Pierre' Sturgeon (who is still a friend today) so I knew that lunacy and anarchy were par for the course!

I actually met the other blokes in the band (Ken and Bruce) when they picked up Pierre and myself at 2:30am to go to Frankfurt. The chick singer Uschi was living there with Harold the manager, which is where we were all to be based.

We spent six weeks doing very few gigs (after big promises) playing at Air bases and discos. After doing three nights in a disco in Hallein in Austria, we came back to Frankfurt and the next day I had a screaming row with 'manager' Harold — who was 'difficult' at the best of times. I was sacked from the band and told to get out of the flat where we were living. None of the other band members stuck up for me and I had to go home from there on the train and ferry, struggling with my guitar, amp and suitcase. Talk about being dropped in the shit from a great height!

When I got back home (after an absolutely hellish journey) I started auditioning again... looking for the 'right' band. One Thursday in the Melody Maker there was another big box ad saying: "Shady Lady need guitarist", well Shady Lady were big on the pub circuit, they had a girl singer who dressed up as a school girl, which certainly drew in the crowds! I went along for a primary chat, at a really flash house in Cuffley, Hertfordshire and after I was short listed, I had a proper 'live' audition and got the gig. The guy I was replacing was Dave Colwell who went onto play with Samson, Bad Company and Humble Pie among others. The drummer Jamie Crompton went on to play guitar (would you believe) with Suzi Quatro and Wishbone Ash! I have heard rumours over the past few years that Jamie is now head of Gibson Guitars in the UK.

We started rehearsing and after a couple of weeks we made a demo at De Lane Lea studios in Wembley, which was a big professional affair. The manager wouldn't put us back on the road until we had got a record deal and things were moving very slowly indeed, so after couple of months, I just thought "fuck this... I want to play live!" so I began to look in the Melody Maker again.

I did a few fruitless auditions and was becoming disillusioned. One night in December 1976, whilst driving home from a night out, a big American car pulled up beside me at the traffic lights (at the junction of Lea Valley Road and Sewardstone Road, Chingford, Essex, to be precise!) When I looked around, I saw none other than Dennis Roy Willcock and two others (Steve Harris and Dave Murray). Dennis recognised me and wound down his window. He yelled out "how ya doin'... you in a band?" "no..." I yelled back." "I'll give you a bell," he shouted, as the car took off like a speedboat into the darkness. Two days later I was in Iron Maiden.

Left: Rehearsing with Moby Dick about March '74.
Left to right: Me, Phil Preston & John Atkins. John 'the Greek' Styliano (keys) is out of shot.

Below: Stone Kerb, May '75.
Left to right: Me, Kev O'Brien, Danny O'Brien (not related... true!)

Below: Nitro.
Left to right: Alan, Vic, me, Dennis & Kev.
(Courtesy Vic Scott)

Nitro, December '75. Left to right: Dennis, me, Alan, Vic & Kev.
(Courtesy Vic Scott)

Snatch, February '76.
L-R; Baz Downes, Danny Hynes and me.
Drummer Darryl Read was, err... hiding!

Snatch about March '76. Left to right:
Danny Hynes, Baz Downes, me and Darryl Read.
Snatch later evolved into NWOBHM darlings Weapon (later, Weapon:UK).

The late Darryl Reed from Snatch.
This guy was an absolute lunatic.
The things him and I got up to are unprintable!

Snatch live in Derby.

IRON MAIDEN AND ME

Two days after the encounter with Dennis and Co. at the traffic lights, I began rehearsing with Maiden in earnest.

These rehearsals took place in the back of a lorry trailer, in an extremely muddy field, tucked away in the wilds of Nazeing, Essex. The field was really a sea of mud and it resembled the "Battle of the Somme" from the First World War. Every night in the dark, after we had all been to work we had to find our way there and wade through the mud in total darkness! On many occasions our cars had to be dug out of this mire before we could go home!

After about a week of this, we had a gig at The Golden Lion pub in London Colney, in deepest Hertfordshire. This was not your average pub gig... it was an event of some sort. Whilst we were setting up the gear, people started drifting into the hall, not your usual rock audience, but men in tuxedos and bow ties and women in ball gowns. There were stares of utter disbelief from both sides and I thought, "we are in serious trouble here". The other act on the bill was a Carpenters style duo with a Hammond organ!

The place was filling up and as they say, "the show must go on" so we went to change into our 'stage gear' in the toilets. I remember saying to Dennis "they are going to kick us of after 30 seconds or they are going to fucking love us!"

I was fortunately right about the latter, after several screaming encores, we had conquered them, even with a PA break down, which gave drummer Rob Rebel a chance to do his 'Derek and Clive' act whilst roadies scampered around fixing leads and things.

Whilst we were changing in the 'bogs', back into our everyday clothes, all these middle aged blokes were coming in and patting us on the back, telling us how great we were and recounting stories of seeing "Hendrix at the Manor House" and "Cream at the Albert Hall" etc... back in the glory days.

Now that the ice was broken, it was back to rehearsing to tighten up the act, as we had been a little 'sloppy' on our first gig. At this stage, I must introduce you to the band – Steve Harris on bass – Ron Rebel on drums (both co-founders), Dennis Willcock on vocals – Dave Murray guitar, and me on guitar. The chief roadie was Vic Vella, a stocky Maltese bloke, who must have been in his late thirties. I'm sure Dennis once told me that he had been a strip club bouncer! There were two other roadies, Bax and Jeff Daniels and also a lighting man, who everyone called 'Dave Lights', as we had our own light show and visual effects... that is, dry ice and a bubble machine (amateur by today's standards but at that time, no other band had stuff like this).

The earliest known picture of this line up (circa; March '77).
Left to right: Dave, Dennis, Steve, me, Ron.
(Unknown)

Our next gig was at the Cart and Horses Stratford on the 1st January 1977. The Cart and Horses was a well know pub rock venue in the East End and back in 1972 a band called Slow Bone, (who I supported in February '72 at the Sirius club, Southgate with Big Ladder Woman) were top band at the 'Cart' and many bands had played there over the years.

From the beginning, the 'Cart' proved to be a great venue. We played there thirteen times in all and each week the crowd just got bigger. After the first three weeks, by 9pm you couldn't get a drink, because they had run out of glasses, such was the crowd. An amusing thing happened every Friday we played there... a phone call would come from another 'Iron Maiden' band from somewhere 'oop north', saying the same old thing... "You have pinched our name, blah blah blah", which proved to be both irritating and highly amusing at the same time. Eventually after thirteen appearances at the Cart (always on a Friday) we were unceremoniously sacked, the landlord was frightened by the size of the crowd that we pulled!

One very amusing incident was when we were playing 'Wrathchild' and Dennis did this little dance. The floor was very wet and slippery because of the soapy water from the bubble machine and whilst doing his dance, Dennis slipped over... arms and legs went everywhere and he landed spread eagled over a monitor speaker! Everyone was in tears of laughter... audience and band alike, I was laughing so hard, I couldn't play, poor old Dennis... his ego took a big hit that night!

Another obscure gig we did around that time was at the South Ockenden Social Club, which was a working mans' club in Essex, not far from Dagenham where the Ford Motor Company had a big factory. How we got booked with our full theatrical act at this

The (now) legendary Cart & Horses pub, Maryland Point, E.15
(Unknown)

place defies belief. I think they regarded us as more of a novelty act than a rock band, but they liked us enough to rebook!

We also played at the Hermit Club in Brentwood in Essex on 24th January — a rainy Monday night. I remember getting to the gig late, because I couldn't find the place, bearing in mind that in those days there was no 'sat nav' or anything and when I did finally arrive, everyone was in a bad mood. On arrival, Dennis said to me "bit fucking late int ya" which really didn't help my mood. The gig itself was not well attended... one, because of the weather, and two, because it was far too remote for any normal follower of the band to find. Because we were all in bad moods, we just went through the motions and got mild applause. Not one of our best gigs!

Another 'outing' on a par with the Hermit Club, was a gig at Central London Polytechnic in Great Portland Street, just north of the West End. It was a student bar and there was literally no interest in us from the start. We were constantly told to "turn down the volume" because these smart kids couldn't talk over us. Despite doing the full act (sword in mouth, blood capsules, dry ice, bubble machine etc) we were treated with total apathy. At the end of the night, I was in the toilet, having an 'eyelash' (slash, that is... a piss), when in walked a couple of students who decided to have a go at me, along the lines of, "who do you lot think your are coming here... with your poofy pantomime act?" We started arguing and getting very intense, when Dennis and Vic walked in and before long, they were getting a serious 'throating' from the three of us. I am sure these two hadn't bargained for this. We learned the hard way that night... don't play student bars if you are, a) not an 'intellectual' yourself, and b) if you want to be listened to!

Going back in time, another amusing outing was when we played at the West Coast pub in Margate, Kent. Back in the 1960s, Margate was a Mecca for Mods and Rockers, a place to meet and fight. I remember going there as a seventeen year old for Easter weekend 1969, with a bunch of mates and sleeping rough in someone's car. All I can really remember was that the atmosphere along the sea front was frightening.

Back to be plot, to do this gig I had to leave work (Ford's factory in Ponders End, Enfield) at midday and get myself round to Vic's in Clapton, East London, which was the rendezvous point. Ron Rebel and I met there, along with Vic, and the rest of the band made their own way to the gig. God knows why.

Ron, Vic and I jumped in the van, a Ford Luton Transit. It only had three seats in the front, as it was a 'box' van. We filled up with diesel at a long gone filling station, just off the legendary Bow flyover in East London, then set off down through the Blackwall Tunnel and onto the A2 towards Margate. You must remember that there were few proper motorways in England in 1977 and it took us hours to get there.

The gig itself went very well, with a screaming encore even! At the end of the night we packed up the gear quickly, as we all had to get home and get up for work the next day. When we were loaded, Ron and I quickly hopped into the front of the van and for reasons unknown, Dennis and Dave got into the back with the gear. Vic pulled down the shutter, which left them in the dark and freezing cold. Ron and I slept like 'babes in the wood' in the warm cab all the way home and when we got back to Vic's at about 3am; we opened the shutters to find them almost frozen to death! Dave was so traumatised he could barely manage a... "fuck that for a laugh" but Dennis was in full flow and reading us the riot act — how could a star of his character be treated like that and never again would he put up with such treatment! Ron and I couldn't stop laughing. I eventually got home at around 4am and had to be up at 7. All the next day I was absolutely knackered but still buzzing from the gig.

After we had been ejected from the 'Cart' we hit the doldrums, we had no gigs to look forward to and somehow acquired the services of a bloke called Paull Sears, a former drummer who I believe Steve Harris had played with in the distant past. He was now acting as our manager and we were rehearsing at Allan Gordon studios in Leytonstone. One night at Steve Harris's Nan's place (he lived with his Nan and not his Mum and Dad for some reason) we were doing an early run through of a new song. There was just Dave, Steve and myself working out the guitar parts very quietly in his bedroom. I can remember saying to Steve, "the main riff of this song sounds a bit funny, I don't think it flows nicely" to which he cut me an icy stare. After that, I learnt to keep my opinions to myself!

At the end of April, the deadlock broke, and we got a gig at the Bridge House pub in Canning Town. Now this pub really was legendary, because every worthy band had played there in the past. People like Rory Gallagher, Paul Jones, Joe Brown, Steve Marriott (one of my all time heroes), RDB, The Pretty Things and even Depeche Mode, and this was just the tip of the iceberg. The Guv'nor, Terry Murphy was a true rock fan. He really appreciated the bands that played at his pub and from what I remember, he was a fucking good bloke, and he liked 'Maiden.

Allan Gordon Studios, Leytonstone, E11 *(Unknown)*

The pub was in a 'no man's land' kind of area... almost under a flyover on the infamous A13 road, which runs from the City of London, out through the East End and into Essex. Without a car, and unless you lived locally, it must have been bloody murder to get to. Yet the place always seemed to be packed. The stage was opposite the bar, with not a lot of distance between them, and with the band's amps and PA facing the bar it must have been a necessity for the bar staff to lip-read!

Maiden always played at the Bridge House during the week and never on a weekend, but we

The legendary Bridge House Pub
in Canning Town, E.16.
(Unknown)

still pulled big crowds. After a few appearances there, we were gathering momentum and rising in status.

Another venue Maiden played, though only twice, was the Plough & Harrow pub, in Leytonstone, About two minutes from Steve's Nan's house. In the early seventies, it really was the place to go. It was packed most nights and at the weekend, the band Powerpack reigned supreme and

Iron Maiden at the Bridge House
(Courtesy Terence Murphy)

had done for years. At our first gig, there was some clown in the audience, who kept shouting out that he wanted to jam with us on harmonica, even though it was obvious that we weren't a jamming kind of band. He made such a nuisance of himself that Vic had to err... deal with him... 'nuff said...

Maiden did a one off gig at the Stapleton Hall Tavern, North London on Monday night 10th May 1977 and were greeted with total apathy for our efforts. None of our normal crowd came, as it was well 'out of area' from the East End and not an easy place to get to. Consequently we never got rebooked not that we particularly wanted to be. As a point of interest, a few years later (1981-1982) I had a band called High Roller and we used to play at the Stapleton every Friday night for months and we used to pack the place! It was a strange venue, a lot of the crowd were 'dodgy' to say the least and we had some very interesting nights there, sometimes barely escaping with our lives! The Governor, Kenny Giddings, (he made the cast of 'Eastenders' sound like Toffs) was an absolute character, a budding guitarist and he absolutely loved our band!

Sorry, back to the plot... At the end of May '77, somehow we got involved in a talent contest of all things, at the Greyhound pub, Chadwell Heath in Essex. The Greyhound was a monstrous venue, tailor made for rock bands and the resident band at the time was Mike Starr and the Starrs, who used to play all the current rock hits. Apparently Mike Starr went on to sing with Colosseum or so the legend goes.

Anyway there was a couple of other rock bands as well as Maiden and a few variety acts as well — magicians, dancers, ventriloquists, etc and we came second to a woman with a talking dog! You couldn't make it up!

Also at the end of May, we got a residency at the Harrow pub in Barking, which is where the East End kind of meets Essex... a kind of dodgy area in those days, plenty of punch ups in the pubs in Barking. This is where the legend of me 'pretending to play guitar with my teeth 'came from. This allegedly came from a lone incident, where, at the climax of our set, Dave Murray and I used to take turns at 'over the top' guitar solos and Dave used to play with his teeth, just like Hendrix did. When it was my turn, I played my bit, bought the guitar to my face, and instead of using my teeth I was doing 'pull off's' on the strings with my hands which meant that you only need one hand to do this trick, the other hand held the guitar up in front of my face so that the crowd couldn't seen exactly what I was doing. Steve Harris spotted me, got annoyed, taking the situation far too seriously and later claimed that I was "not being true to the fans", or words to that effect. This one incident sparked off a myth which seems to have become part of Iron Maiden folklore... crazy eh?

Around this time — mid '77 — it was Queen Elizabeth II's Silver Jubilee and the East End of London, being traditionally a very 'patriotic and proud to be British' area had many street parties to celebrate. Us Maidens were invited to play at one in Teviot Street in Poplar London E14. On the day I found it very difficult to find the place, which was in a big housing estate with a Square, buried in the bowels of the East End, with a stage and canopy built for us to play under. I barely got there in time bearing in mind there was no street map or sat nav. All I had was a black and white A-Z of London to find my way about with. Poor old Ron had the same problem, in fact we had to start the set with Paull Sears playing drums for a couple of numbers before Ron arrived but all went well and the crowd loved us! There are some good black and white photographs of us at this gig knocking around somewhere courtesy of Dennis.

****

Maiden at the Teviot St. Bash.
(Courtesy of Dennis Willcock)

The only time Maiden ever supported another band was when we supported Trapeze at the Music Machine, Camden Town. The venue was originally an Edwardian Music Hall and was a great rambling building, with many balconies and passageways. It was a great place in the mid to late seventies with a great atmosphere; all the top bands of the time played there and Trapeze were certainly one of my favourites. They had been around for a long time and released many albums (all of which I have) and I was dead keen to play on the same bill as them. I thought Maiden might be in with a chance of 'blowing them away', rather stupidly, as I had seen them a week previously at London's Roundhouse where they were definitely not on top form.

Back to the actual gig... We had to set up our gear, right at the front of the stage, leaving us very little room to 'strut our stuff' and so as to make a dramatic intro, we decided to start with the powerful instrumental 'Transylvania'. Ron counted us in... one, two, three, four on the high hat and as

Dave and I tore into the opening riff, things began to go badly wrong... Dave's guitar kept crackling loudly and cutting out. We had to stop and start three times before Vic discovered that Dave's guitar lead was falling apart! We eventually got going, but we had hopelessly lost our edge and momentum, we never recovered throughout the set and quite frankly, up against Trapeze, we looked like a bunch of amateurs.

We had successfully blown our 'London debut' and went home licking our wounds, and vowing that a situation like that would never happen again. To cap it all, Trapeze were brilliant that night. We lost a lot of face with our East End fans, who had come especially to see us. I personally wanted the fucking ground to open up and swallow me, I felt that ashamed.

Two days later it, was business as usual, we were back to reality playing a return gig at the South Ockenden Social Club. We continued our Bridge House and Harrow Barking residencies until we were asked to headline at the Tram Shed in Woolwich, South London, which had just been refurbished as a rock venue. The band supporting us were called Va-Va-Voom. Not being 'metal' or even hard rock, they were completely miscast and even though they played well, our followers gave them a cold reception. We however, had regained our momentum, and went down a storm. There is an iconic photo of me at this gig, made famous for the pink snakeskin boots I was wearing! People who have seen this photo have apparently been amused by the great platform boots (very fashionable in their day) and personally I blame Dennis for taking me to this boot shop in Holloway Road, the place where he got all his stage boots, and some of his were far more outrageous than my pink ones!

Something interesting I must mention... all our fees for playing these pubs were around £20-£25 which was not a fortune at all in those days and as all this money got consumed with expenses, there was none left for us

personally afterwards, but I think we must have broken even at the Tram Shed. We were paid £40 and believed we were on our way to the big time!

On Monday 18th July we played the Bridge House in Camden Town and unbeknown to me, this would be my last ever gig with Maiden. For on the Thursday of that week, at about 7:15 pm there was a knock on my front door. I opened the door to find

Vic and Dennis on my porch, dropping off my amp and stuff. "Whats going on?" I said, or words to that effect. Dennis replied "err... there has been changes in the band... and, err... and you're not in it anymore," before the pair of them disappeared back into the van and off into the distance. I was totally shocked, speechless. I had spent seven months with Iron Maiden and we had done nearly fifty gigs together. I was convinced that it would last forever. I found out later from Ron Rebel, that Dennis and Steve Harris had wanted me out for being "too flash" on stage and also found out, that on the same night, they had done the same trick to Dave Murray. I heard that the reason for his demise was that his girlfriend and her mates irked Dennis for some obscure reason!

With Dave and myself gone from Maiden, Dennis drafted in his old mate Terry Wapram from Hooker and soon afterwards, Ron Rebel was also ejected and replaced by Barry "Thunderstick" Purkis.

A while later, they recruited Tony Moore on keyboards. Tony had played in Tanz der Youth with Brian James from The Damned and also the Cutting Crew, at some point in his varied career. This line up didn't last very long, maybe one or two gigs, before things changed in the Maiden camp once again...

Left: Dennis and I at large!
Above: Me in full flight.

Some pics from the 'Cart, early '77 taken on an old Kodak!
You can tell from our 'stage clothes' that it was the seventies!
Those bubbles (from our trusty bubble machine)
were the reason for Dennis's mishap!

Steve & Dave.
Steve's gold strides were almost as bad as my pink snakeskin boots!

Above: At the Cart early '77. I actually bought that top I was wearing!

Left: With Dennis at the same venue.

Above: Dennis in full flight, at the 'Cart.

Right: Ron Rebel at the same venue.

FOR IRON MAIDEN TRAIN SPOTTERS: EQUIPMENT LIST

ME
1968 Gold Top Gibson Les Paul
Antoria Flying 'V' Guitar
Fender Twin Reverb Amp

DAVE
Fender Stratocaster
Wine Red Gibson Les Paul
Marshall Master Volume 100 Head, and Angled 4x12 Cab
Wah Wah pedal

STEVE
Fender Jazz Bass – Sunburst
Various Amps, including:
Peavey Head – H & H Valvestate Head – Very Rare
Transistorised Hi Watt Head
Marshall Reflex Bass Cabinet

RON
5 Piece Black Hayman Drum Kit
Zildjan Cymbals

PA etc

Not entirely sure what the PA was, but we had a big mixing desk and monitors and it was about 500 watts of power. We also had various lighting effects — a dry ice machine, a bubble machine and Shure microphones.

The Van was a Ford Luton Transit.

As well as Vic there were two other roadies — Bax (John Baxter) and Jeff Daniels.

Dave' Lights' Beasley controlled the lighting effects and Vic Vella was driver, humper and minder. He still works for the Iron Maiden Industry after all these years!

I have to admit, that for a good while after my 'departure' from Maiden, that I was pretty sore about how I was treated, considering all the hard graft that I'd put into the band but, as they say, 'all is fair in love and war... and rock 'n' roll!'

I still to this day maintain my friendship with Ron Rebel and have recently (September 2014) been reunited with Dennis Willcock. But until the reunion in July 2004, at the Cart and Horses, Stratford, to film the bits for the 'Iron Maiden- Early Days DVD', I hadn't seen any of the Maidens since their first headlining tour, summer 1980.

Ron Rebel later played briefly with a jazz rock band called Blitzfish and later on, with John McCoy and Bernie Tormé and at one time, with the late Paul Samson. Until recently he and Terry Wapram played in the band called The Space Chickens. Ron also played in Gibraltar with Dennis Willcock in early 1981 but that's another story entirely...

IRON MAIDEN'S GIGS
(during my time with them)

1976
Sunday 19th December Golden Lion, London Colney, Hertfordshire
(private function)

1977
Saturday 1st January   Cart & Horses, Stratford, East London
Friday 7th January   Cart & Horses, Stratford, East London
Saturday 8th January   South Ockendon Social Club
Friday 14th January   Cart & Horses, Stratford, East London
Friday 21st January   Cart & Horses, Stratford, East London
Monday 24th January   Hermit Club, Brentwood, Essex

Friday 28th January	Cart & Horses, Stratford, East London
Friday 4th February	Cart & Horses, Stratford, East London
Friday 11th February	Cart & Horses, Stratford, East London
Friday 18th February	Cart & Horses, Stratford, East London
Friday 25th February	Cart & Horses, Stratford, East London
Friday 4th March	Cart & Horses, Stratford, East London
Saturday 5th March	Central Polytechnic, Great Portland St, London
Friday 11th March	Cart & Horses, Stratford, East London
Wednesday 16th March	West Coast, Margate, Kent
Friday 18th March	Cart & Horses, Stratford, East London
Friday 25th March	Cart & Horses, Stratford, East London
Thursday 28th April	Bridge House, Canning Town, East London
Thursday 5th May	Bridge House, Canning Town, East London
Tuesday 10th May	Stapleton Hall Tavern, Crouch End
Thursday 19th May	Bridge House, Canning Town, East London
Monday 23rd May	Harrow, Barking, Essex
Saturday 28th May	Harrow, Barking, Essex
Monday 30th May	Plough & Harrow, Leytonstone, East London
Thursday 2nd June	Bridge House, Canning Town, East London

BRIDGE HOUSE   23 BARKING ROAD CANNING TOWN, E.16
Thurs. 2nd: **IRON MAIDEN**

Saturday 4th June	Wapping Festival
Monday 6th June	Plough & Harrow, Leytonstone, East London
Tuesday 7th June	Teviot Street (Silver Jubilee party)

IRON MAIDEN

Thurs., 2nd: THE BRIDGEHOUSE, CANNING TOWN, E.16
Fri., 3rd: THE HARROW, RIPPLE ROAD, BARKING
Sat., 4th: WAPPING FESTIVAL, WAPPING PARK, E.1
Mon., 6th: THE PLOUGH & HARROW, HIGH ROAD, LEYTONSTONE, E.11
Tues., 7th: TEVIOT STREET JUBILEE PARTY, E.14

"You ain't seen nothing yet!"

Wednesday 8th June	Bridge House, Canning Town, East London
Friday 10th June	Harrow, Barking, Essex
Saturday 11th June	Harrow, Barking, Essex

Friday 17th June	Harrow, Barking, Essex
Saturday 18th June	Harrow, Barking, Essex
Sunday 19th June	Bridge House, Canning Town, East London
Thursday 23rd	Music Machine, Camden Town (supporting Trapeze)

Saturday 25th June	South Ockenden Social Club
Sunday 26th June	Wapping Festival
Monday 27th June	Plough & Harrow, Leytonstone, East London
Friday 1st July	Harrow, Barking, Essex
Saturday 2nd July	Harrow, Barking, Essex
Monday 4th July	Bridge House, Canning Town, East London

Friday 8th July	Harrow, Barking, Essex
Saturday 9th July	Plough & Harrow, Leytonstone, East London
Monday 11th July	Bridge House, Canning Town, East London
Tuesday 12th July	Tramshed, Woolwich
Friday 15th July	Harrow, Barking, Essex
Saturday 16th July	Harrow, Barking, Essex
Monday 18th July	Bridge House, Canning Town, East London

BRIDGE HOUSE 23 BARKING ROAD CANNING TOWN, E.16

ALL ADMISSION FREE

Thurs. 14th:	THE RETURN OF SOME OLD FRIENDS
Fri. 15th / Sat. 16th	ZAINE GRIFF AND SCREEMER
Sun. 17th	JACKIE LYNTON AND HAPPY DAYS
Mon. 18th	IRON MAIDEN
Tues. 19th / Weds. 20th	FILTHY McNAUGHTY FEATURING CHRIS THOMPSON

IRON MAIDEN ARE NOT ONLY THE <u>BEST</u> VISUAL, HIGH ENERGY, <u>ORIGINAL</u>, LOUD BUT TALENTED, GOOD LOOKING, TASTEFUL, HEART-BREAKING, HARD HITTING, BLOOD SUCKING, MIND BLOWING, <u>HARD ROCK BAND IN LONDON</u>! WE'RE ALSO VERY NICE BLOKES, KIND TO FANS & OUR FAMILIES, HOSTILE TO OTHER BANDS, BUT ABOVE ALL WE'RE BRILLIANT, ACE SUPERSTARS & WE'RE HONEST! & WE'RE **BACK!!!!!!!** SO FANS, RECORD COMPANIES, AIR MEN, AGENTS, PROMOTERS, FINANCERS & ABLE YOUNG LADIES, <u>WATCH THIS SPACE FOR DETAILS</u>!

Dennis at the Cart & Horses.

Ron Rebel.

ON THE ROAD WITH PRAYING MANTIS

After the demise of Slow Motion, my last band in December '78, I had been out of a proper band for just over a year. I had been to hundreds of auditions and been offered a few jobs, but nothing really seemed to be happening. The only place to look in those days was in the good old Melody Maker. It was the only music paper that bands and musicians advertised in for new personnel. If you weren't 'in the know' and I certainly wasn't, it had to be the dear old Melody Maker. I used to religiously toddle up to the newsagents in Ponders End High Street, early on a Thursday morning, to get my copy, in the hope of getting lucky, but after a year, my enthusiasm was running very low.

After Christmas '79, when all the festivities had run their course, it was time to resume my quest. All I wanted was to join a half decent band and gig again. I didn't even think of stardom. The very first edition of Melody Maker in January 1980 contained a box advert saying, "Praying Mantis seek Guitarist". I'd heard the name and knew that they were a NWOBHM band gigging at some interesting venues. As soon as I could find some time on my own at work, (at this time I worked as an engineer, repairing and installing gaming machines, that is fruit machines, space invaders, juke boxes and pool tables etc), when I was alone in the workshop I rang the number on the advert. No answer... "Please leave your name, experience, equipment etc etc and we will call you back". I know now that my 'ace card' was mentioning that I had been in Iron Maiden because less than an hour later I got a call back from a certain Jeff Crook, who was their manager at the time. We chatted and he said that the band knew Maiden. The next thing I knew, I was being given an audition time and the address of a school in Cable Street, Stepney, East London, the scene of some heavy political riots in the 1930s. The audition was set for a Sunday morning! Jeez... what rock musicians are alive on a Sunday morning? Blimey they must be serious!

I think that I actually didn't get pissed the night before and went to bed at a reasonable hour on the Saturday night. I set off next day in my battered old Mini van and eventually found the place, got parked up and wandered into the school and immediately heard the drone of a rock bank down the corridor. I had bought with me, a newly acquired black Les Paul Custom guitar that as rumour had it, had once belonged to Micky Moody of Whitesnake. I hoped it would bring me luck.

The previous 'contestant' shuffled out of the door and as I went in, the band greeted me. Chris Troy on bass, Tino Troy on guitar and Mick Ransome on drums. Hand shakes all round. "You the bloke from Maiden?" says Tino. "Yeah" I replied. Steve told us about you. "Anything good?" I said, trying to break the ice. "Yeah... Oh yeah." Tino said casually.

They showed my one of their songs, Tino counted the band in and away we went, me following and adding guitar fills here and there. This went on for about an hour and when we stopped playing, we all had a chat and got on very well. We all had the same silly sense of humour, which in the past had been the 'clincher' as to whether you got the gig or not.

When I got back home, I was absolutely praying (no pun intended) that I would hear some good news about my audition and what seemed like weeks later, the phone rang (it was actually about 6:00 pm the same day). It was their manager Jeff (later to be christened "The Jefference" by me, as I have a penchant for stupid nick names and school boy humour). He said that the boys would like me to join the band. I don't know if it showed in my voice, but I nearly passed out with joy. I couldn't believe it. After all this time in the wilderness, I was at last allowed back into the arena.

When rehearsals started in the same old school in Cable Street, it was evident that this was to be a 'professional' venture. There was a tour planned, which was the "Metal For Muthas "tour and other assorted gigs, so I had to be available pretty well every day, which meant my job at Dillow Amusements had to go. I held on until the last second before I gave in my notice and much to my surprise, Melvin the guv'nor, was very understanding and supportive. When I told him why I was leaving, he said, "if it doesn't work out come back!" I couldn't believe my ears.

The rehearsals began in earnest and I must admit, I found it quite hard to take in the complexities of the songs which were all originals written by Chris and Tino but I did my homework and made sure I was on top of the situation.

The tour was called "Metal For Muthas" because it was specifically to promote the soon

> ## Maiden pull out
>
> **IRON MAIDEN**, who lined up a month-long tour through February two weeks ago, have had to postpone all dates from February 13 as they're going into the studio with producer Will Malone to record their first album.
>
> Mallone, who has previously worked with Black Sabbath and Meat Loaf, is only available for the last part of February and early March and so the group will reschedule the postponed dates for April and May, after they've finished recording and toured with **Judas Priest** as special guests on their tour. Mallone has also produced Iron Maiden's first single, 'Running Free', which is released by EMI on February 15.
>
> For the dates through the first part of February, Iron Maiden will be joined by fellow 'Metal For Muthas' band **Praying Mantis** and Heavy Metal Soundhouse DJ **Neal Kay**.

to be released album of the same name from EMI, the whole thing being instigated by a certain heavy metal DJ called Neal Kay.

Neal Kay was (for a small bloke) was a 'larger than life' character. He looked like the cartoon character, "Hagar the Horrible" and he had, as they say, 'more front than Harrods'! His enthusiasm for heavy metal was boundless and on top of that, a fucking good bloke and a real character! He and fellow DJ Tommy Vance pretty well spearheaded the NWOBHM, for without them; it would never have been anywhere near as successful as it was... in my humble opinion.

At this point I must mention that it was Neal Kay that championed Maiden. They had given him a demo and he absolutely loved it. He sang their praises so loud, that various record companies took notice and when Maiden got Rod Smallwood as their manager, there was no stopping them... and there still isn't to this day.

Back to the plot — Praying Mantis had roughly two weeks rehearsal and now it was time for the tour to commence! The back line gear had been taken care of by our manager Jeff and our roadie Lee Burrows, who had been with the band for quite a while prior to me joining. We, the band, had been instructed to assemble in the Swan pub, Hammersmith Broadway, at approximately 2:30 pm on the 30th January 1980. Much later than 2:30, Vic Vella, Maiden's minder come roadie turned up in a mini bus, swearing profusely (in a Maltese accent) about the traffic. By this time, we all had had too much to drink and I for one, was feeling the worse for wear. We all piled into the mini bus and we were told that we were going to Shepperton Film Studios for a pre-tour rehearsal. Fucking hell! I I have hit the big time! After arriving at Shepperton, all our gear was set up on a gigantic stage, in what looked like an aircraft hangar. We started to play through our set and I could see Clive Burr and Paul Di'Anno from Maiden fucking about and purposely making a nuisance of themselves. I had only just met these two clowns and I knew that between the three of us there would be some gross stupidity in the near future.

The sound in this place was cacophonous. It sounded like everything was louder then everything else. We had to turn the volume down considerably to get a listenable sound. This a valuable lesson we learnt in how to play in big venues, that is let the PA system make you sound loud, you don't need to be that loud on stage with a big PA. That way you can hear the monitors, which means you can hear your vocals, very important when trying to sing harmonies!

When we had finished, Maiden went on for their turn. Christ, I thought we played loud at first but their volume was stripping the paint off the walls. Unlike us, they didn't turn their volume down, they just carried on regardless.

I needed a break from this racket and needed an "eyelash". When I eventually found the "khasi" (toilet), which was miles away, I was suddenly overrun with loads of dwarves dressed in outrageous clothes! What the hell was going on here I wondered? I later found out that they were filming *Time Bandits* a surreal comedy starring Sean Connery and John Cleese, among others!

When Maiden had had enough of rehearsing, the gear, theirs and ours, was loaded into a big truck which crawled off into the night. For us, our roadie, Lee Burrows, the "Jefference", lighting crew et all, we climbed aboard an old Bedford coach, ready to begin the seventeen-hour slog to the first venue... Aberdeen University in Scotland.

The journey was endless. It seemed as if the driver was going as slow as possible on purpose. He seemed to take the old country route, that is to say, not using any motorway known to man. We had numerous stops for 'nose bag' (food), and an "eyelash" and "big jobs" (relieving oneself if you please!) The boredom was really setting in, we all played 'I spy' for hours and there is only so much piss that can be taken out of other motorists, before it becomes clichéd. On top of all that, sleep was impossible, because there was always some twat who just had to poke you and wake you up for no reason. And of course, the constant breaking of wind, (that developed into an Olympic sport!) that kept everyone amused.

Friday 1st February: Aberdeen University

We eventually arrived at Aberdeen University (17 bloody hours later) and found that the gear had got there, hours before, (which was hardly surprising and was set up for sound check. As Maiden were headlining they had first go. As I mentioned earlier, they did their rehearsal at Shepperton... err... rather loudly, so for a little peace, I had to leave the building, along with many others who didn't need to be there. We all went to a local cafe for 'nose bag' and afterwards, generally wandered about. Two hours later we returned to find that the noise had stopped and the band were just lurking about on stage, mumbling to each other. After a few minutes of this they all sauntered off, and it was our turn. Bearing in mind it was now about 7:30pm and the doors were opening at 8, we thought we had better look sharp. So sharp in fact, that because of our lesson learnt at Shepperton, we were all done and dusted by 7:50 because we didn't play loud... job done! The secret of a good sound check is to get your sound levels right, do a couple of songs and leave it at that, don't overdo it, get off whilst you are on top! While we were wasting time pre-gig, Dave Murray and I were in the dressing room and he was showing me his guitars. One was a black Fender Strat, which he had newly acquired, he told me where he had got it. I put two and two together and realised it was the same guitar that the late great Paul Kossoff of Free had owned. It was originally a white maple neck '57 Strat, but Dave had had it bastardised beyond belief! He'd had it sprayed black and put Dimarzio humbucking pickups on it. Absolutely sacrilege! If that guitar had been left in its original condition, it would now be priceless. However, Dave used it as his main guitar for years and I believe he still has it to this day.

We are called to battle stations by Neal Kay announcing that "Praying Mantis will be on stage any second." Christ... we were still putting on our stage clothes and tuning up in the dressing room, hardly ready for action. We were very quickly ushered up on stage, to a tepid cheer and I hit the first chords of 'Rich City Kids'. I was shitting myself but after the first couple of songs, my confidence was there and I really got into it. We came off to a full cheer! I had done my first gig with Praying Mantis and was feeling far more confident. The others in the band were pleased with our performance and moral was high!

It was now Maiden's turn, they came on stage to a big cheer; their reputation had been spreading like fever across the country. Their opening number hit everyone with such force that you could physically feel the pressure of the volume. The kids loved it and each song drew more applause than the last. I watched for a while and then went outside for some fresh air, along with others from our entourage. Maiden finished to a deafening cheer and left the stage, waving to the crowd, who were fanatically waving back. Ironically (no pun intended) they were not happy with their performance and were arguing profusely in the dressing room among the mayhem of people there... all tucking into free sandwiches and beer, provided by the promoter. The ice was broken, my 'baptism of fire' and now, I felt I was ready for the next onslaught...

Saturday 2nd February: Glasgow University

After leaving Aberdeen Uni in the early hours of the morning, we drove through the night to Glasgow... a bloody long journey in almost total blackness, and believe me, it was a long cold boring night. I think I slept for about half an hour max, as I was so fired up from the previous night's gig. As we crawled into Glasgow in the early hours, the place was covered in snow. While we crept through the run down suburbs, it looked like I would have imagined Chicago to have looked in the depression in the 1930s.

We got to the venue very early and had to wait ages to be let into the hall. It was freezing cold outside and as we had 'nosebag' laid on. There was no need to go out of the building, so most of us stayed inside. At the sound check I noticed that my new Les Paul Custom kept feeding back. I hadn't used it on the previous gig as I had used my old Les Paul Standard that I'd had for years, so I thought that tonight I would use this one for a change. It seemed like the pick-ups were microphonic, which means that at certain gain and volume levels from the Marshall amp, I would experience uncontrollable feedback, which pissed me off no end. I had talks with the roadies about it as they were

used to problems like this, and they couldn't work out why it was happening. In the end the general consensus was that some guitars are dogs and some are not, so it was back to my trusty Standard for this evening's gig.

After the sound check we all put our feet up in the dressing room (not for very long) and after changing into our stage gear, we strolled on stage. The gig itself was good, the audience loved us, and I could already feel that I was gelling with the band and getting more comfortable with the songs and feeling more at ease on stage.

Sometime later on in the tour I swapped that black Les Paul with Dave Murray for a Gibson Explorer 2. He really liked the Les Paul and it didn't seem to bother him at all about the sound problems and I was quite happy with the Explorer, as it was a guitar I had never had before.

Maiden played a blinder that night and despite some heckling, which Paul Di'Anno swiftly dealt with, they were rolling like a well-oiled machine. Den Stratton (along with Clive Burr) were, like me, relatively new boys, and I could see that they were feeling their way into Maiden's set pretty well. The mood in the dressing afterwards was really positive; both bands were on a high. Things were beginning to look very promising!

Sunday 3rd February: St Andrews University

After another long crawl through a cold dark night, we arrived about midday, after stopping at the motorway services. You must bear in mind that back in 1980, motorway services were nowhere near as sophisticated as they are now. One bloke took the order, cooked it, took the money and then served the food, so you can imagine how long it took to serve us lot. And whilst the poor sod was trying to cater for about fifteen or so hairy rockers, we were stuffing our faces with everything we could lay our hands on, and of course not paying for anywhere near as much as we had scoffed!

At the venue, the gear was still being set up, so as usual we had lots of time on our hands. We discovered that the place had a sauna so we just had to sample it. Now, the only problem with having a sauna, is that it makes you very relaxed and lethargic. By the time it came to doing the gig, we were so comatose, we could hardly keep our eyes open. It must have been the most lifeless, laidback live performance ever done by a rock band! It was as much as we could do to stay awake! However, the audience loved us, god knows how or why. We found out later that our manager the "Jefference" (his surname was Crook!) was at the bar talking business with Rod Smallwood, Maiden's manager. Talk about out of his depth, he made "Delboy" look like Sir Alfred McAlpine. He was a lovely bloke, but he was the most "professional amateur" that I had ever come across!

Just to elaborate on the "Jefference", he had been with Praying Mantis for a few years since their pub rock days. He was in his late twenties and he looked about forty-nine. He was extremely loyal to the band and originally he had put a lot of his own money into keeping the band afloat. He looked like a 1950s B movie actor and he came from Colchester!

Monday 4th February: Tiffany's, Edinburgh

After yet another sleepless slog through the night to Edinburgh, we got there to find that the venue was none other than a disco, not your usual rock venue, but a John Travolta style disco.

While the gear was being set up, I noticed that there was something missing from the general noisy antics, Clive's voice was not heard like it usually was. This intrigued me so I went off in search of him. I eventually found him sitting in a corner, with his feet on the table with a bloody 'spud gun'. Those things you had as a kid, that you dug the barrel into a potato and fired by compressed air. He was taking pot shots at the decor and anything else that was fair game! We all thought this was a jolly good wheeze... only brought to an end when the rest of the Maidens decided to play football. The ball was being kicked at anything and anyone and all manner of things were getting knocked over. This was all brought to a sudden halt when Rod Smallwood appeared. He seemed bemused by the childish antics that had been occurring.

The gig itself was good for both bands but it took time for Maiden to build up steam. Paul Di'Anno was getting irked by the lack of response and after a few numbers he came out with an utter classic comment, along the lines of "...can you lot fart? 'Cause if you can, it's got to be fucking louder than your applause!" which drew a wall of laughter from the crowd and after that they were sailing and finished to a deafening roar!

For some reason it seemed to take forever for the crew to dismantle the gear and load the truck. That night we didn't get away until about 3am.

Tuesday 5th February: Public Hall, Grimsby

After that late getaway from Edinburgh and about an hour's drive into the darkness, horror of horrors... the bloody coach broke down in the middle of nowhere! You have to bear in mind, that this was years before mobile phones were invented so there was precious little means of communication in a situation like this. The poor old driver "Captain Compass" as he was called, had to walk miles in the snow to find a phone box to call for help and it took about six hours for the 'cavalry' to arrive, by which time most of us, if not sleeping, were virtually bored to death and starving bloody hungry.

Once the coach was fixed, we sped off trying to make up for lost time. When we arrived at the gig, it was like the roadies worst nightmare. The place had a stepped stage, great for public meetings etc, but certainly not for a rock band (or two) with vast drum kits and amps etc. Grown men were falling to their knees in tears with cries of utter disbelief, but the show must go on. So out came saws, hammers and timber and the like, and literally everybody set to work to make it possible to get stacks, drums, and all the rock paraphernalia assembled for tonight's show. When it was finally ready, sound checking was done with surprisingly military discipline (for a change) and all was in readiness.

Then came the next drama. Paul Di'Anno (by now my burgeoning partner in crime) decided that his voice was shot, and that there was no way he could sing, no matter what. After all that had happened, Steve Harris was fucking adamant that Maiden would play, and he declared that if Paul wasn't going to sing then he would! After all, he knew all the lyrics. I don't believe he had ever sung in his life before but he did it. It was a most interesting performance and he got a lot of respect from all of the entourage... not least the audience. I think Paul was shocked to think that he would do it, but Steve Harris would never let anything stand in the way of a Maiden show going ahead. That is why over the years Maiden has been so successful.

Our set was pretty lack lustre, as we were all knackered for obvious reasons, and when we went on, most of the crowd were in the bar, no encore for us that night.

Wednesday 6th February: Romeo & Juliet's, Bristol
When we got to the venue once again it turned out to be another bloody disco. While the roadies were setting up the gear, and because of the way things were going, we knew that it would be hours before we got a look in and because some unknown person had booked us a bed and breakfast for that day, we could have some rest and freshen up, so we took the opportunity.

After a good kip, we had a bath and a hair dyeing session (Tino and I decided to 'Henna' our hair for that red 'rock star' look). Now this 'Henna' stuff is a powder and when mixed with water it goes like cow shit and it feels like sand in your hair. The problem is you cannot seem to wash it out, your hair constantly feels gritty. We also ruined all the towels in the room doing it; they all ended up brilliant red so we hid them before we left. That's enough of our beauty secrets!

We got a taxi back to the venue (god knows who paid, as we were all skint) and Tino, for a complete wheeze, decided to talk absolute gibberish to the poor taxi driver. It was such nonsense that he was coming out with that we were all biting our hands to stifle the sobs of laughter and this poor driver was baffled (to say the least) and Tino kept a straight face throughout!

When we got to the venue we told Paul and Clive, who thought it hilarious. Den Stratton and Loopy (one of Maiden's road crew) just looked at us and shook their heads in polite disgust.

We actually got a long sound check (half an hour!) this time so everything looked good, unfortunately the gig was not that well attended, much to the surprise of everyone, but Mantis tore into their set with growing confidence and we got a well deserved encore. Maiden however appeared to be going through the motions and from the wings I could see a displeased look on Steve Harris's face, and at one point it appeared that Steve and Paul were arguing between songs. Maiden nevertheless finished to a big cheer and played a hearty encore but back in the dressing room there were voices of discontent. Us Mantis boys just hit the free booze with gay abandon and let them Maiden boys argue it out.

Thursday 7th February: Unity Hall, Wakefield

We boarded the coach at about 2:30 am in the freezing cold for the next haul up to Wakefield Yorkshire, which compared to some of the distances we travelled was relatively nearby.

As well as being tired, Tino was feeling decidedly unwell, he had his head in a plastic bucket for most of the journey, spewing, or 'blowing chunks' as we used to call it, and I was wickedly sniggering at his plight, something that would backfire on me at a later date.

We finally got to Wakefield and eventually found the hall and luckily found an unused room, so all of us poor knackered Mantis boys could lay down on the floor to try and get some much needed sleep as sleeping on the coach with all the high jinks had been an impossibility.

At the sound check nothing went right, absolutely nothing. I was dreading the gig, and so were the others.

Showtime! Oh Christ... must we, we all thought? Neal Kay, always upbeat, announced us and a great unexpected cheer went up. Instantly we were all charged up and tore into 'Rich City Kids' which was our usual opening number, with real venom. We just went from strength to strength and the set got better and better. They demanded an encore and we tore into 'High Roller', a new song of mine that we were trying out and they were screaming. They loved the acapella bit and were all singing along. The gig was far better than we expected. We trooped off stage in a state of euphoria.

Maiden on this occasion absolutely tore the place apart — they played like demons. The applause hurt your ears, Paul's voice was certainly back on form and he was letting them know it. Another screaming encore and he was at his cocky best, and Steve Harris's face was beaming. Back in the dressing room after the gig, the atmosphere was amazing, everyone from both bands was on a massive high and we couldn't wait for the next onslaught.

Friday 8th February: Polytechnic, Huddersfield

Tonight was Huddersfield Poly. Now we all knew that we had to make a real impact (in as many ways as possible) because this was Rod Smallwood's hometown. Both bands were checked into a really sumptuous hotel (once again, I really cannot fathom who paid for our stay, as we were living on thin air at this time). After checking in, we all realised that we had most of the day to kill, sound checks were hours away so mischief must be found.

Tino, Paul, Clive and I decided to go 'shopping'. We went

up and down the high street, in and out of all the shops, generally making a nuisance of ourselves. When we tired of this we went back to the hotel for a drink.

Now, when I say it was a "sumptuous" hotel... it was far too good for the likes of us, it had flock wall paper, grandfather clocks, suits of armour and stags heads mounted on the walls, and was filled with proper business men, all in suits: Faceless, chinless wonders — all with two point four kids and little houses in the greenbelt. Heads turned and mouths fell open when us four walked in, all with our long hair, scruffy jeans and black leather biker jackets.

Paul had the "are you looking at me?" look on his face and we eventually got served at the bar (after all the bar staff did their very best to pretend that we were in visible), the boozing and the loudness began in earnest.

After about an hour, we were becoming very 'oiled' and the language, especially from certain quarters (no names mentioned) was becoming so purposely bad, that these "suits" were leaving in droves, until we at last had the bar to ourselves. I must admit sometimes I swear profusely, but even though I was pissed, I was embarrassed by this behaviour. Somehow (I can't quite remember exactly) Tino and I staggered back to our room to sleep it off for a couple of hours. Christ knows what happened to Paul and Clive.

When we did eventually get on stage at the gig, Tino and I both felt dreadful as we were still pissed and getting through the set was an ordeal, but we must have played alright as the audience demanded an encore!

The Maidens set that night didn't seem to suffer from any signs of drunkenness from certain quarters and they played a magnificent set, much to Rod Smallwood's delight!

There was apparently a big after gig party but I felt so rotten that all I could do was stagger back to the hotel and crash out.

Saturday 9th February: Manchester University

This was supposed to be a big gig on the tour for some unknown reason, but the gig was attended not by "Metal fans"... well maybe a few, but mainly by students. Arrogant little bastards (remember the Maiden gig in March 77 in a North London Polly?) both bands played well to a general wall of apathy and indifference. During Maiden's set, Paul was throwing out some great sarcastic quips addressed to "the jury" in between songs and dealing with hecklers with a stock phrase "if you don't like it, why d'ya fucking come? We're getting paid anyway... so bollocks to ya!" The only good thing for me anyway was that some friends that I hadn't seen for a long time were able to come along and we had a drink afterwards in the bar. I certainly do not wish to play there again... ever.

Sunday 10th February: The Lyceum, London

We were driving through the night (as usual) from Manchester to London. I remember being wide-awake whilst the rest of the chaps on the bus were out for the count. We were all supposed to stay in a hotel (or doss house) in Kings Cross, or somewhere just as hideous, but as the band neared London, I collared the driver, and talked him through a detour, so that he dropped me at Finchley, within walking distance of my girlfriend (now wife's) parents house. I told him the way back to his proper route, but something must have gone horribly wrong.

When we all assembled at the Lyceum the next night, Rod Smallwood came stomping over to the Mantis crowd with a face like thunder! He rounded on me screaming "you selfish little bastard. All because of you, they got lost and it took hours for that poor fucker (the driver) to find the hotel! Don't ever do that again, you understand!"

Our entire crowd, girlfriends included, looked on in utter disbelief. I felt like a naughty schoolboy! The rot was beginning to set in. Rod was seriously narked with yours truly.

Another incident that also fuelled the fire, took place at one of the earlier gigs. The dressing room at this venue, was the student common room and it was completely at both band's disposal. After the gig, I remember, along with certain nameless factions of the Maiden ensemble, we were in very high spirits after drinking serious amounts of free lager and things began to get sillier by the minute. Every time a bottle was finished, the empty would be slung (in true rock 'n' roll

A press cutting for the Lyceum gig.
As it happens, this is where
my Mum (as a young teenager)
saw Glenn Miller during WW2.

hooligan style) around the room, and food was also being slung about with gay abandon. The room was in a right mess. When we'd all tired of this, we decided to look for more mischief and trouped off down the hall, to what looked like a gym changing room. Whilst I disappeared for an 'eyelash' the others had obviously found another form of 'entertainment', because I heard an almighty crash. Christ knows what they'd done, but something had seemingly been trashed. The general view was, "Christ we are in the shit now!" Then we heard footsteps outside, we all ran in different directions, and in the distance, I could hear Rod Smallwood screaming, "who the fuck did this!" I am bloody sure that I heard Paul say something like "it was Bob, he started it all (snigger, snigger). The reality was, that we were behaving like delinquent schoolboys on a school trip, fucking about the whole time, the only difference was, we were all in our twenties and old enough to know better!

Monday 11th February: Civic Hall, Mansfield

This was the last gig on the tour and it was great for both bands. As for the Lyceum the previous evening a third band was added, Diamond Head, they were first on, and at every opportunity, their singer (a budding Robert Plant) kept whinging about them not having a sound check. I thought, "For Christ sake mate, we have done a complete tour without a proper sound check!"

Anyway back to the plot. After terrible trouble finding the place, I don't know why because the driver found every venue okay, the gear got set up but there was precious little time for any sound checks (what's new). The infamous DJ Neal Kay got the crowd warmed up and I particularly remember them going absolutely mental when he played Molly Hatchet's 'Boogie No More'. I have never seen head banging like it.

The reception both bands got was good, but it was bit of a low-key end to the tour, as there were no 'incidents' to recount, which really should have finished at the Lyceum.

Ladies and gentleman... so ended Iron Maiden's and Praying Mantis's first ever British Tour.

As an interesting 'trivia' point, whilst Maiden were recording their first album, around March, 1980 at Kingsway Studios, in Holborn, London, us Praying Mantis chaps were in the area one afternoon and decided to drop in on them.

This is Wil Malone's album released in 1970. It sold a mere handful of copies at the time but now it can go for around £2000. Blimey!

The most amusing person there was their producer, a guy called Wil Malone. He had been in a legendary late sixties band called Orange Bicycle and had also released a solo album (which I later acquired and is now worth a fortune because of his Maiden connection). The reason he was so amusing, was because of his err... attire. He was wearing what blokes wear on a trawler... a full Sou'wester outfit... in a fucking recording studio! And he had a big 'ZZ Top' beard!

He didn't speak much to any of us, which was hardly surprising, as we took the piss out of his clothes constantly!

This gig was cancelled, it became part of the main tour.

This gig was cancelled, it became part of the main tour.

PRAYING MANTIS: BETWEEN THE TOURS

Friday 29th February: 76 Club, Burton upon Trent
Our first gig after the tour was the 76 Club, a real dive, situated deep in the Black Country. We played our balls off to a half-hearted crowd; however, there were a few people that did like us. Luckily, we stayed in a B & B next door to the venue, so there was no journey home though the night, with the driver fighting to stay awake. With this as an added bonus, we were allowed free booze after we had played. We all crawled downstairs to breakfast the next morning, nursing serious hangovers from the previous evening's indulgence, before the long crawl home...

Saturday 1st March: Raven Hall, Corby
The Raven Hall was a gigantic function room on the back of a pub. The stage unfortunately was only about a foot high, and barely deep enough for a drum kit, this meant that we were right at the very front. The crowd that night were all well and truly "rocky" and they were right in our faces. One young headbanger was dangerously close to me, and as he was rocking back and forth in a trance like state, he accidentally "nutted" (i.e. head butted) my guitar, right on the point where the fingerboard overlaps the body. Now Gibson Les Paul guitars are pretty heavily constructed and although I really felt the whack of the collision, the guitar sustained no damage, the poor sod who nutted it simply disappeared from

view. That was the last I saw of him! I hope he recovered. The gig came to a screaming end, and they bloody loved us, which gave us a buzz throughout the long night home.

The next three gigs we had were supporting Nazareth, a well established, no nonsense band of Scots.

Wednesday 5th March: Norwich University

We got there early in the afternoon and Nazareth were sound checking, whilst we were unloading our gear. As we waited by the side of the stage, I noticed that I knew one of the roadies, a certain Steve Casey, who had worked with none other than UFO, The Pretty Things, Hawkwind and too many others to mention. Years before, we both worked at the same GPO factory in Enfield! Talk about a small world. We had a good gig that night and Nazareth were superb.

Thursday 6th March: Queensway Hall, Dunstable

The Queensway Hall was a strange place. On the inside it was oval in shape and the walls were lined with wooden planking, needless to say the reverb (when the place was empty) was outrageous but once the place filled up, the sound was fine and both bands had a good gig — and a good piss up afterwards on the free booze.

Friday 7th March: Mayfair Ballroom, Newcastle

After the Dunstable date, we had to travel overnight to Newcastle. Chris Troy was driving and he, like the rest of us, was asleep on his feet, (or at the wheel). Somewhere up North, in the early hours, we hit a patch of black ice. Luckily there was nothing else on the road because we spun like a top, thankfully coming to a halt unscathed (but in the middle of a roundabout). This certainly woke us all up!

When we got to the venue, we were chatting to Nazareth and told them about our "skidding" incident and they were most concerned. As we got to know them, it transpired that they were damn good blokes (I had heard this before from my mate 'Pierre' Sturgeon who had supported them back in 1973 at Torquay Town Hall). Just before we went on for our set, Manny Charlton, their guitarist came into our dressing room armed with various bottles of wine and said, "here lads, get stuck into these and when we have played come into our dressing for a real party." Bloody good blokes eh! We played to a great reception and so did the Naz and, as invited, we trooped into their dressing room and boy did the booze flow. Before we were too pissed, Tino and I were talking to Manny about guitars, amps and just about everything to do with rock 'n' roll. He had an arsenal of heavily modified Strats and he also had an early Boogie combo as a tune up amp. With the alcohol flowing we got well and truly silly. Just before I crashed out, I remember wrestling on the floor with their bass player Pete Agnew. He looked more like a pro-wrestler than a bass player! But it was very playful and we were like long lost mates.

On the drive home some serious hangovers were once more being endured. After this we had a few days off... our next gig was...

Wednesday 12th March:
The Music Machine, Camden Town, London

Because we had been on a Nationwide Tour (err... eleven dates) and done a string of one nighters across the country, we thought that this, our first London gig since the Lyceum, would be a guaranteed full house. Wrong! The support band, a certain White Spirit, all the way from the North East, had brought with them coach loads of supporters and when they finished their set (to thunderous applause) more that half the audience vanished! We played a half-hearted set to a handful of mates and passing punters. Talk about back to earth with a bang!

Thursday 13th March: Drill Hall, Lincoln

On this gig we were supporting Girl (a glam metal band that contained Phil Collen, later in Def Leppard and their singer Phil Lewis, later in LA Guns). We had never met them before, but within minutes, we were all dead matey and swapping stories about guitars and gigs and stuff.

When we had both played, we descended on the free drink in the dressing room for a good session. We then told them we had better head home, as we had nowhere to stay (and precious little money). Phil Lewis was having none of this and demanded that we go back to their hotel and doss down there. That seemed like an excellent idea.

On following them out of town to their digs, we all took a detour to a late night service station-cum-transport café. This place was almost deserted, except for the one poor sod who worked there. He had to take the orders, cook the grub and take the money, all on his own. Bearing in mind that with both bands and roadies etc, there must have been about fourteen of us and this poor bugger was totally overwhelmed! By the time we got to paying, we had eaten our way down the line, and with bulging chops, proceed to pay for, say a cup of tea and a Kit Kat (having scoffed about four sandwiches and umpteen cakes each). While we continued to eat at the tables, someone thought that it would be a good wheeze to pelt the poor café worker with soggy teabags. What a laugh! Only it didn't stop at teabags, everything we would lay our hands on got slung at him! In total desperation, he ran into the back and promptly called the old bill! Needless to say we had a police escort (and a severe caution) back to their hotel!

Friday 14th March: The Lafayette Club, Wolverhampton

I remember us crawling up the M1 on a grey, rainy Monday afternoon, and having extreme aggro finding this place. We eventually got there, set up and sound checked by late afternoon. It was a real dive of a place. I had heard stories of what a shit hole it was from many musicians... and yes they were right. I had seen tacky discos in need of a serious refurbishment, but I don't think this place had been touched since the early sixties.

What should we do now? Some bright spark came up with a brilliant idea. We would play "outings" with the lights out! Outings as I am sure everyone knows, is a kids game, where you all hide except one person who has to find everyone else — as people get found they join in to get the others, obviously the last one caught wins!

Playing this game when you can see what you are doing is one thing but in total darkness, it is a fucking riot!

We must have lost track of time (having so much fun) because the bar staff began to drift into the place, however we just carried on playing, to their complete bewilderment!

The gig itself was an anti-climax. I think three men and a dog turned up! But we got paid and being philosophical about it as they say, you gotta take the rough with the smooth.

Saturday 15th March: Technical College, Hitchin

Because this was a fairly local gig, I drove myself in my old heap of a Mini van. We were on the same bill as our mates Girl. We were all in the dressing room, swapping rock 'n' roll stories, when somewhere decided to de-bag "The Jefference". As we all tried to grab him, he lashed out (as you do) and a blind kick caught me right in the bollocks. I went down like a sack of shit. Everyone stopped, as I lay writhing and swearing on the ground. Oh Gawd! We were due on stage in about five minutes! I hobbled on and Christ knows how I got though the set, because I could hardly stand, let alone throw myself about. The next day I went to the doctors, who did all the usual stuff, holding my aching nuts and telling me to cough etc. All he really said was take things easy!

Friday 21st March: JB's Club, Dudley

This club in Dudley just west of Birmingham was a legendary place. It has been a rock venue since the late sixties and all the great bands of that era (e.g. Free, Mott The Hoople, Slade, Trapeze, Man and Humble Pie to name but a few) had trod the boards there. The place itself was little more than a tin scout hut (no disrespect intended). Our set was received well but not rapturously, as the audience had seen it all before.

Saturday 22nd March: City Hall, St Albans

On this gig we were supporting the Pat Travers Band, who were pretty well established. While both bands were sound checking and getting acquainted, we were enthralled at Pat Travers back line. They were the first band I ever saw with their Marshall amp heads removed from their wooden cabinets and built into a rack, years before "racks" were commercially available. Also their guitars (both Pat Travers' and Pat Thrall's) were fitted with early Floyd Rose tremolo systems. Tino and I were talking to them for ages about their gear and allsorts of music stuff. They were really nice blokes, their road crew however were a different matter. They all had massive egos and were very loud. I also remember talking with some other musos from the audience, before the gig started, when the late Paul Samson (from the band Samson) appeared. From what I gathered, he wasn't very popular in some quarters and someone threw in a snide comment about him, to which Samson barked back, and verbally cut this bloke to shreds! The gig though was pretty good, but the Pat Travers Band really kicked ass.

Monday 24th March: Romeo & Juliet's, Birmingham

The previous night Melinda and I had been to the Golden Lion in London to see a band and meet up with my old mate from Snatch (and later on Weapon) Danny Hynes and a few others. We ended up at Danny's flat, just around the corner from the pub, and I got seriously pissed. I kept insisting that I would be alright to drive home (what!) when all of a horrible sudden, I was violently sick on his floor before crashing out! I woke up on Danny's floor the next day, feeling utterly vile and thinking, 'oh Christ I have to get home to get my gear, as I am playing in Birmingham tonight!'

We said our goodbyes and Melinda shovelled me into the car. I had to take her home to North London first and then get to Enfield. Unfortunately, just as we got to the Thames Embankment, the car overheated. We were all dressed up in our rock 'n' roll attire just as the office folk were driving to work! The car needed a drink badly (it had boiled over), thank fuck for the river! I had an empty bottle in the back, and filled it from the Thames! God knows how, but I managed to get us home, because I was still technically pissed from the previous evening. When I got in, I just had time for a quick bath and to gather my stage clothes together, before the chaps were banging on my front door.

I slept all the way there and we finished our sound check by late afternoon. As this place was right next to the Bull Ring (a notorious shopping centre smack in the middle of Birmingham) we decided to go for a coffee.

I have never been into such a foreboding place as this. Police in riot gear with Alsatian dogs were breaking up the gangs that were loitering there and as we were totally the opposite of the locals, with long hair and fancy clothes, there was a lot of hard staring and teeth sucking! We made a quick exit!

The gig itself was a non-event. Never in the field of human conflict, have I played to such an overwhelming wall of total apathy. So we all looked forward to the long drive home...

Friday 28th March: The Village Club, Newport, Shropshire

Talk about an out of the way place for a rock venue. I think they had only just got of rid of steam trains! We arrived eventually and waited, and waited for the PA chaps to arrive. With barely an hour to spare, they turned up, giving us every excuse under the sun for their lateness and we all worked like maniacs to get everything up, assembled, and working. I don't know why we bothered. By 9:30, there were about four people in the place. We came a fucking long way to play to four people, but as the late Spider Clarke (bass player in the mighty Big Ladder Woman, one of my earlier bands) once said "a gig is a gig... and it must be done!"

Monday 31st March: Genevieve, Sheffield

We set off well early and all of us (PA boys included) got there with hours to kill. We did a nice long sound check and once again thought, "we know a good game." The lights went down and a serious game of "outings" commenced. There were eight grown men here, playing a kids game and it was fucking brilliant! As before at Wolverhampton, the clubs staff began to arrive and couldn't believe the stupidity and childishness that they were greeted with!

Before we went on, we met Pete Willis and the late Steve Clarke of Def Leppard at the bar and had big chats: All of us being proudly part of the NWOBHM. There was also another celebrity present...

At the bar, along with his entourage, was a well-known comedian from the early seventies, none other than Charlie Williams. Now let's bear in mind, Charlie Williams was a black man but his jokes were extremely racist (you have to remember political correctness was light years away!), so nobody took offence. He had this catch phrase, "ey'oop flower!" and after we played we all gathered round him at the bar making his life a misery, mimicking him, his jokes and the phrase in our drunken state. He chose to leave fairly quickly after that. We had a brilliant night (about time, to). The crowd loved us... well worth the trip to Sheffield.

Sunday 6th April: Town Hall, Cheltenham

I spent the whole journey reading a new book that I had recently bought: 'Rock Family Trees' by Pete Frame. Being a complete anorak about rock music history, it seemed as if this book had been written especially for me and I dreamt of having my name included in a future edition. We arrived at the gig to find that we were being supported by Sledge Hammer (who were also on the *Metal for Muthas* album). We had never seen a venue to equal this place. It was a Victorian town hall made completely of marble. At the sound check, because the place was empty, the natural reverb was like playing in the Grand Canyon. We just gave up and hoped and hoped the place would be filled at the time of the gig to soak up the noise. Unfortunately it wasn't — half full maybe.

Consequently both bands sound came over as an absolute din, punctuated by screams. I do vaguely remember us being a bit snotty towards Sledge Hammer (I don't remember why). The gig itself went well, except for me having a problem with my pedal board. I did a typical theatrical moody and kicked the mic and stand into the audience, which made them think Christ what's he going to do next. Nothing like a bit of rock 'n' roll petulance to keep them interested!

Maiden run free

IRON MAIDEN, touring with Judas Priest at the moment, follow that and the partial success of their 'Running Free' single on EMI with a massive tour and the release of their debut EMI LP.

The album, 'Iron Maiden', will be previewed at the Kingsbury Circle Heavy Metal Soundhouse on April 6 and in the shops on April 11. Tracks include the single plus live faves 'Prowler' and 'Phantom Of The Opera' and it was produced by Will Malone. The first 25,000 copies will be sold at the special price of £3.99.

The tour, which features **Praying Mantis** as support and **Neale Kay** as DJ, is as follows: Lincoln Drill Hall May 15, Newcastle Mayfair 16, Ayr Pavilion 18, Aberdeen Music Hall 19, Carlisle Market Hall 20, Bradford St George's Hall 21, Withensea Grand Pavilion 22, Cambridge Corn Exchange 23, Dunstable Queensway Hall 25, Blackburn King George's Hall 27, Wolverhampton Civic Hall 28, Hanley Victoria Hall 29, Swindon Brunel Rooms 30, St Austell New Cornish Riviera 31, Bristol Locarno June 1, Malvern Winter Gardens 2, Portsmouth Locarno 3, Cardiff Top Rank 4, Cromer West Runton Pavilion 6, Birmingham Odeon 7, Sheffield Top Rank 8, Liverpool Royal Court Theatre 9, Sunderland Mecca Centre 11, Glasgow Apollo 13, Middlesbrough Town Hall 14, Wakefield Unity Hall 16, Leicester De Montfort Hall 17, Chatham Central Hall 18, Guildford Civic Hall 19, Bracknell Sports Centre 21, Brighton Top Rank 22, Manchester Apollo 26, Bath Pavilion 27, Oxford New Theatre 28, Swansea Brangwyn Hall 29.

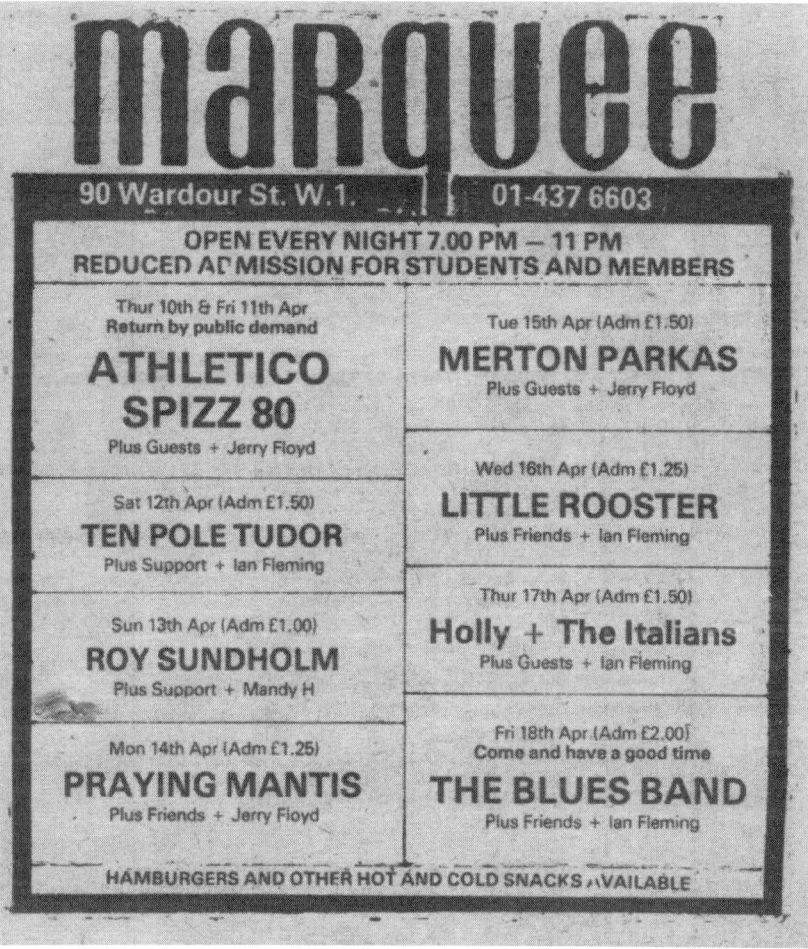

Was this cancelled and put back to May?

Friday 2nd May: Marquee Club, London

I had waited many, many years to play this venue and all our mates and prospective "management" team came to see us. After spending all afternoon perfecting the sound, we played a brilliant gig and consequently had "professional" management on the horizon.

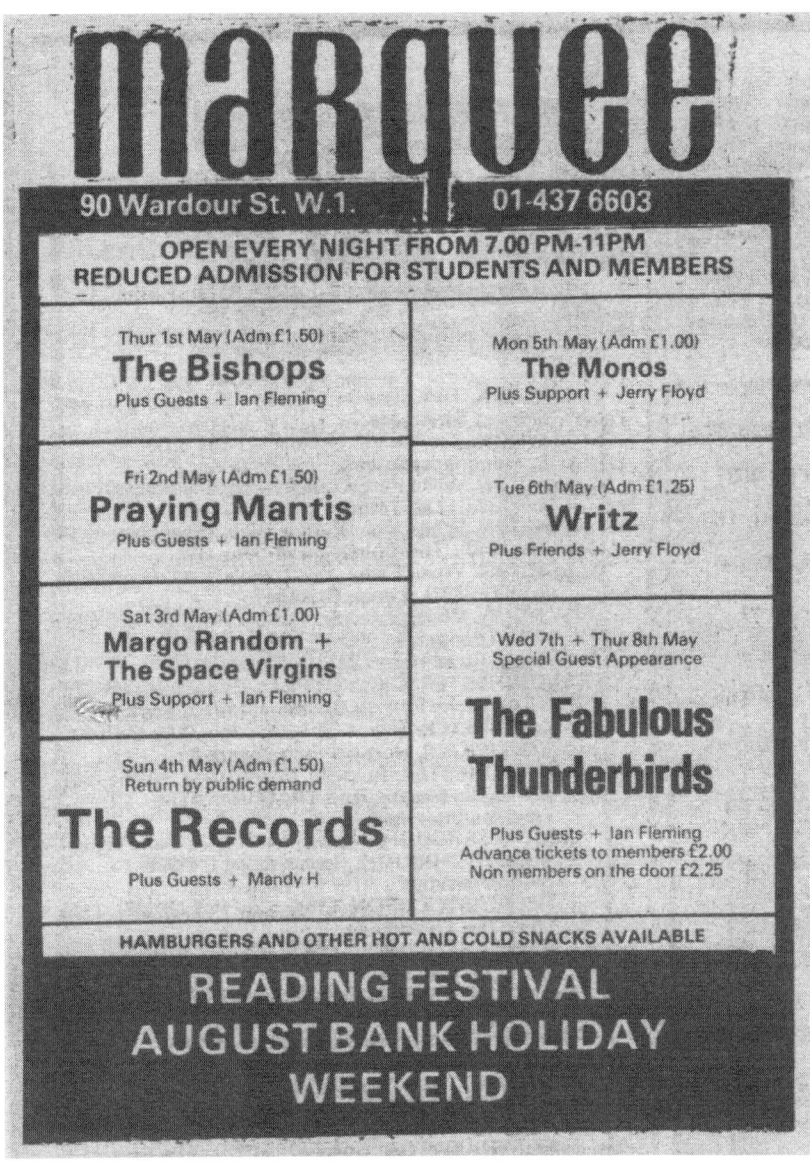

THE PROFESSIONALS GET HOLD OF US!

Our new 'management' slid their way in and the poor old "Jefference" (Gawd bless 'im) became instantly redundant. I know that Tino and Chris felt really bad about this as they had been friends for a long time, however, in this game, poor innocent bastards are routinely trodden on.

The first thing they did was to get us to do a showcase gig at a studio in Smithfield, London. A certain ex-pop star and entrepreneur, Mr. Dave Dee, of Dave Dee, Dozy, Beaky, Mick and Tich fame came along to see us. He arrived, hand shakes all round and said, "just play through your set", so we did. When we got to my song, 'High Roller', he said he liked it and he also particularly liked 'Rich City kids' which Tino and Chris had written. All the other songs had also been written by them and he thought them very good. But he thought 'High Roller' was maybe a little "too commercial". Anyway, what happened next was all a bit vague and we eventually signed too GEM Records (the same label as Samson).

Within days we were installed at Wessex Studios in Highbury, North London. I was extremely impressed by us recording there, particularly because King Crimson did their milestone first album there, back in 1969, which incidentally is one of the greatest progressive rock albums ever recorded... no sorry the greatest. I must add at this point, that the management thought that Mick Ransome, our drummer was not really suitable, which was a shame, because he was a great bloke. We began auditioning new drummers; among the candidates were Les Binks, formerly of Judas Priest, and also Reg Isadore, formerly of the Robin Trower Band (he played on the magnificent *Bridge of Sighs* album). We decided on a guy named Dave Potts, who had a long history of experience dating back to the mid sixties. He had previously played with: The Crying Shames, Mandrake Paddle Steamer (who I had seen many times as a youth — a truly great progressive band) Ten Years Later (with Alvin Lee) and The Ray Thomas Band (the Moody Blues guy). Christ what a fucking track record. I personally was proud to have him aboard.

With Dave in the drum chair things really began to come together. After intensive rehearsals, we decided to record the song 'Praying Mantis' with 'High Roller' as the B-side. A mate of Tino's and Chris's produced it, called Alan Leeming. He had been a tape operator on a Moody Blues session and now fancied himself as a record producer. After the recording at Wessex, the single was mixed at Marquee studios, above the aforementioned club in Wardour Street. Sadly the end result sounded like a bloody demo. The best thing about the record was the cover, done by a certain Rodney Matthews.

We were due to start the Iron Maiden headline tour (six weeks solid on the road!) on 15th May, so we had to get into shape. Our new management ('Fireball Management' actually) decided that we should have pros working with us, so Pete Bennett (ex-Savoy Brown) was recruited as back line man and minder and Kenny Smith (ex-Emerson Lake & Palmer) became our stage manager. The ace in the whole, was Bob Adcock as tour manager. This bloke had been with (wait for it)... the Mersey Beats, Cream (throughout their legendary American tours), West Bruce and Laing, Rainbow and finally, The Scorpions! We were indeed not worthy! I felt severely humbled to be in this guy's presence, he was a really nice bloke. I used to sit wide-eyed listening to the tales of all the bands he had been with. I had to keep pinching myself.

Now that we had professionals on board, we were not living on a shoestring as before. That meant that bills and expenses could be met properly, although we were still living on a pittance. "If you don't sell records you don't earn" and we had a long way to go.

IRON MAIDEN

ALBUM OUT NOW

£3.99 RRP LIMITED EDITION

Featuring

PHANTOM OF THE OPERA · IRON MAIDEN · TRANSYLVANIA · PROWLER
CHARLOTTE THE HARLOT · REMEMBER TOMORROW · STRANGE WORLD
Plus Re-mixed version of 'RUNNING FREE'

SEE THEM ON TOUR

MAY
15 LINCOLN Drill Hall
16 NEWCASTLE Mayfair
18 AYR Pavilion
19 ABERDEEN Music Hall
20 CARLISLE Market Hall
21 BRADFORD St. Georges Hall
22 WITHENSEA Grand Pavilion
23 CAMBRIDGE Corn Exchange
25 DUNSTABLE Queensway Hall
27 BLACKBURN King Georges Hall
28 WOLVERHAMPTON Civic Hall
29 HANLEY Victoria Hall
30 SWINDON Brunel Rooms
31 ST. AUSTELL New Cornish Riviera

JUNE
1 BRISTOL Locarno
2 MALVERN Winter Gardens
3 PORTSMOUTH Locarno
4 CARDIFF Top Rank
6 CROMER West Runton Pavilion
7 BIRMINGHAM Odeon
8 SHEFFIELD Top Rank
9 LIVERPOOL Royal Court Theatre
11 SUNDERLAND Mecca Centre
13 GLASGOW Apollo
14 MIDDLESBOROUGH Town Hall
16 WAKEFIELD Unity Hall
17 LEICESTER De Montfort Hall
18 CHATHAM Central Hall
19 GUILDFORD Civic Hall
21 BRACKNELL Sports Centre
22 BRIGHTON Top Rank
25 DERBY Assembly Rooms
26 MANCHESTER Apollo
27 BATH Pavilion
28 OXFORD New Theatre
29 SWANSEA Brangwyn Hall

EMC 3330 on EMI Records & Tapes

THE MAJOR OFFENSIVE: MAIDEN'S FIRST BIG TOUR

By most standards this was a major tour. Six weeks in length, with about four days off. England expects every man to do his duty...

Thursday 15th May: Drill Hall, Lincoln

The tour began in earnest here. We had played the Drill Hall two months earlier, supporting Girl. This time it was the real deal. Capacity crowds. Great expectations. We had to hit the ground running, and we did. We had the crowd right from the 'off'. We couldn't put a foot wrong! A great reception (almost as good as Maiden's). We had broken the ice.

Friday 16th May: Mayfair Ballroom, Newcastle

As previously mentioned, we had played here with Nazareth. It's always wise to know a venue beforehand. It was another great night, another great crowd. Both bands enjoyed a lot of humorous banter. The booze flowed freely afterwards with many pats on the back for everyone. One particularly silly stunt that occurred here was when, at the soundcheck, Clive Burr appeared on an old Roadster pushbike that he had 'found' outside. He was riding it around the hall, hooting and hollering (as usual) and of course, Paul wanted a go on this bike. Within minutes, everyone had to have a go on the bike, and at one time, there were about six of us all perched on it and the poor thing was bending and buckling under the weight! By the time we'd all finished with it, it was totally fucked... both wheels bent like figure eights, so we sneakily put it back from whence it came.

About an hour later, the caretaker came screaming into the hall, demanding to know what the fuck had happened to his bike! Everyone went quiet, all except for Paul, Clive and me. We were trying desperately not to laugh out loud, but our sniggering gave us away. This bloke then rounded on us and by then, he had a face like a gargoyle. The more he ranted, the more we laughed. In the end, Uncle Rod stepped in and pacified him with a promise of a new bike. Rod then turned to us three...

Saturday 17th May: Kinema, Dunfermline

As a point of trivia, Dunfermline is Nazareth's hometown (I just thought I would add that).

There was an incident before the gig. Something to do with Maiden's tour manager, Adrian. No one seemed to really know what it was about, but he was starting to be proving a right... err... diva? It was also Paul Di'Anno's 21st birthday, so as I am sure you can imagine, a piss up ensured after we had finished playing.

We had a particularly good gig that night, for some reason, they really loved us, Maiden being over loud, (as was often the case), still received a rapturous response.

Sunday 18th May: Pavilion, Ayr

Ayr Pavilion is a cavernous place, it must have inspired Marc Bolan to write the song 'The Ballrooms of Mars', after playing here, which he must have done at some time. Following the sound check, I wandered around the place alone, marvelling at the sheer size and splendour of it. Back to the plot, Neal Kay (who was DJ and "master of ceremonies") introduced us and I ripped into the opening riff of 'Rich City Kids'. Tino whacked a chord on his guitar and nothing... silence. We all stared at each other with a "fuck me... what now?" look on our faces. I knew that I had to bluff the rest of the number, so I turned it into a short instrumental, and finished it prematurely, as the roadies scampered about behind the amps. Not a good start, but with Tino's gear now working, we tore through the rest of the set with a vengeance and won a screaming ovation. At one point during the set, someone kept launching balloons at me and to be clever, I was kicking them back into the crowd, whilst not missing a note (we all like a clever bastard don't we!) Maiden's set was monumental that night — Paul Di'Anno was on serious form and had the crowd in his hands. He would have given David Lee Roth a run for his money. Even Steve Harris was pleased!

Following the gig, we were starving and took off into the night and found a Chinese take away. The grub was taken back to our hotel and we promptly demolished it. In the early hours, I woke with an excruciating bellyache and before long I was spewing violently into anything available. Eventually there was nothing left to come out of me, but water. I felt like I had been tortured by the Spanish Inquisition and the Gestapo at the same time... completely wretched. The bad news was, we had a gig that night in St Andrew's, a four-hour drive away. Now that we had the "professionals" behind us, we had our own mode of transport... a Ford Transit Caravanette of all things. What a ridiculous vehicle! We all called it the "Hot Dog Van" because that is what it looked like.

Monday 19th May: Music Hall, Aberdeen

At about 10:00 in the morning, we set sail for the next gig at Aberdeen and because I was still so ill I climbed into the overhanging bit in the cab, a bed of sorts, armed with a large saucepan (stolen from the hotel in Ayr), a spewing receptacle. Bob Adcock, our well-travelled tour manager, had a formula one racing license and proceeded to drive accordingly.

Despite my fragile guts, he was slinging the van around mercilessly going around roundabouts on two wheels and literally driving the thing like a speedboat! When we finally arrived at the venue I felt so unwell and dizzy that I wanted the last rites and just to be left to die. I felt like I couldn't stand, let alone play, but I didn't want to let the chaps down. I was so weak backstage that the sound check went ahead without me. I had to be dressed by the others and Tino tuned my guitar and hung it on me. It felt like a bloody anvil around my shoulders. We walked out into the wings of the stage as Neal Kay went into his big build-up, "and now from London... Praying Mantis!" The place erupted with a deafening roar. I have heard of adrenalin and all that, but Christ, I felt like I had been plugged into the mains! The rest of the band were amazed that this feeble, 'sick as a dog' guitarist, had changed from Jekyll into Hyde in an instant. I stormed on stage and we played like Roman gladiators, the cheering after each song was louder than the last. Everyone knew how ill I had been and were visibly shocked at my transformation. Immediately after I left the stage the wretchedness returned. Back in the dressing room, there were numerous pats on the back,

The author. An advert for Marshall Amps?
(Courtesy Freddie Silva)

however when Bob Adcock said "well fooking dun, la' (in a proper Scouse accent)" I was a tad choked because this bloke was a serious rock 'n' roll veteran.

Later the rest of the lads went on the piss, but Bob took me back to the hotel first for a well-needed early night. I must have slept for about ten hours but the next morning I felt fine and ready for the next encounter.

Tuesday 20th May: Market Hall, Carlisle

Many people have said... don't ask me why... that Carlisle is the arsehole of England. The only band of any renown to come from there was Spooky Tooth, who were quite superb, (I saw them live in 1969 and they were a fucking power house).

The Market Hall was a great mausoleum of a place, the ceiling was so high and so was the stage (not that I mind that).

After the day before's escapades and the blinding gig we

had, I had a feeling that this one would be a disappointment. No one was in a particularly good mood. Paul Di'Anno was descending into prima donna mode and Steve Harris was beginning to show his displeasure. The gig itself was not good. A poor turnout (possibly the worst so far) and a problem with the mains supply, meant that as soon as either band ended a song, there was a loud hum from the equipment... not good.

The 'digs' we stayed at that night, would not have looked out of place on an early *Coronation Street* set. The landlady even looked like Ena Sharples and those who did not eat their breakfast were made to!

Wednesday 21st May: St George's Hall, Bradford

Yet another Victorian monstrosity of a building. The sound check for Maiden was an awful din in this colossal, echo chamber of a place. Therefore when it was our turn, we made sure we did it quietly. We were done inside twenty minutes. We made it our rule that if the sound check went well, don't over do it. Don't go through the whole set unless there is a need to rehearse something particular. When the venue filled up and the stage lights were lit, both bands gave a rousing performance and everything was all right.

The only thing of note was after the gig, when 'certain factions of the Maiden contingent' had an altercation with the caretaker over an unseen occurrence in the corridor (i.e. something either got nicked or smashed or both). Right... the bloody lot of you outside the headmasters room this instant!

Thursday 22nd May: Grand Pavilion, Withernsea

I had never heard of Withernsea or its whereabouts until this day. It is actually on the Yorkshire coast, near Hull.

When we got there the gear was nowhere near set up so the road crew told us all to 'piss off' for a few hours, and we did. I don't know where the Maiden mob went, but the other three Mantis boys and Mr Adcock went over the local park to play football. They all loved football but I fucking hate it. They would often do this if we had time to spare in the afternoons. I would take the opportunity to wander around the town 'shopping' and looking for second hand guitars or record shops (you never know what goodies you might find). On this occasion I saw an old Watkins Dominator amp for £25 in an old back street junk shop. I wished I had brought it, because years later I began to collect vintage amps, and this particular model would be worth over £1000 today (if you could ever find one).

We returned to the venue at around 5:30 and the roadies had the right hump as the hum problem was back, only worse. However, the show must go on, so we played our set, but this hum was seriously off putting and although we went down well, we were seriously narked. For Maiden it was worse because of their volume although the crowd didn't seem to notice it — probably, because their ears were well and truly bludgeoned by the sheer volume.

Later on some smart arse said, "lets all go for a Chinese!" We (me especially) took a chance and fortunately, there was no reoccurrence of my previous... err... 'misfortune'.

Friday 23rd May: Corn Exchange, Cambridge

Once again a Gothic Citadel! The Ceiling was even higher than what had gone before. I know loads of bands that had played here, but I was particularly intrigued, because the legendary Syd Barrett (of the early Pink Floyd as everyone should know) played here in 1972. His band Stars was supporting the legendary MC5, which, in comparison, is like Marc Bolan taking on Mike Tyson.

Next door to the place was a burger bar and throughout the afternoon various personnel frequented it, the reason being that the burgers were the nearest thing you could get to those served at the Hard Rock Café in London, i.e. mega tasty!

We played our set and I am sure I noticed guitarist Tony McPhee (of the Groundhogs) milling about in the crowd, much to my amazement. It was another memorable gig and I was particularly pleased, because the onstage sound was shit. In the dressing room afterwards, there was much praise from the management.

Maiden took to the stage and the audience came surging forward, despite the intense volume, kids were actually standing inside the giant bass bins, headbanging, oblivious to the damage being caused to their internal organs. Paul Di'Anno was in his 'ska/mod' mode that night, wearing a pork pie hat, Crombie and loafers. This engendered seething disgust from Steve Harris. The writing was once again on the wall.

Whilst this was going on our management team asked if we wanted to go for a meal, and if so where? Someone suggested Peppermint Park. Peppermint Park is in the heart of London's West End, whilst we were in the heart of Cambridge. That's around forty miles away, is it not? All eyes were on Bob Adcock. "No problem," he says, already slipping on his driving gloves.

Within minutes, we were tearing out of town and onto the M11. Honestly, Adcock could have been a stunt driver for the *Dukes of Hazzard*. I am sure we arrived before we actually left!

At Peppermint Park we posed as 'rock stars' and filled our bellies with burgers (again), along with booze and cocktails, all at GEM Records expense. After making complete and utter pigs of ourselves, most of us fell unconscious in an alcoholic haze.

Luckily we had a day off next day, which enabled us to recover, and boy did we all need it.

Sunday 25th May: Queensway Hall, Dunstable

Another venue we had already played on the 'Metal for Muthas' tour. As I have said before, it was that strange, oval shaped building, with the wood planked walls. I think that bloke who designed must have been on drugs. Or if he wasn't, he should have been.

Whilst waiting for the crew to assemble the 'artillery', I found myself exploring, and discovered that it had an upper floor. With me was the ubiquitous Mr Di'Anno, always on the lookout for some mischief. Alas we could find none. That is, until Paul spotted a passer by outside through a large upstairs window. Opening the top half, he began to shout and holler at the bloke below, and when he had got his full attention, he quickly dropped his trousers, and bent right over... spreading the cheeks of his bare arse against the glass. The bloke stood there, looking in disbelief for a moment and then shook his head and walked away. The delighted Di'Anno pulled up his 'strides' chuckling and giggling dementedly, as he strode down the corridor to find the others to tell them of his latest stunt.

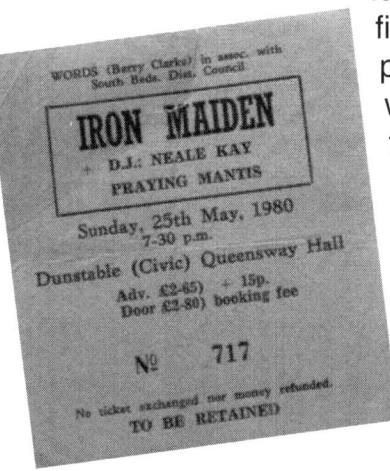

The gig however, was lifted from going through the 'going through the motions' level, to the "lets now fuck about" stage, when someone in the audience blew up a couple of johnnies (condoms) and began to bat them about in the crowd. Inevitably they reached us and we of course joined in the fun. There were more that a few bum notes and missed vocal lines because we were hitting and kicking these 'dunkies' around. Despite this tomfoolery and sloppy playing, much to our amazement, we got an encore.

After we'd finished our set, us Mantis boys buggered off to find somewhere 'exotic' to eat, missing the Maiden's set entirely, but everyone said they put on a great show.

Monday 26th May: Assembly Rooms, Derby
The only thing I remember from this occasion was a near death experience (i.e. a close fucking shave). Whilst sound checking, a telescopic lighting column became unstable because a stay wire had broken. This resulted in it coming crashing down inches behind me. Everyone was transfixed. If I had been a foot further back, I wouldn't be writing this now. I think I got through the gig in a state of shock. The same thing happened to the great Curtis Mayfield, only the poor bugger was actually crushed, causing him major injury.

Tuesday 27th May: King George's Hall, Blackburn
When we arrived, everyone was milling about backstage, so I thought I would try out my latest wheeze which was hooking people together. I had heard about T Rex drummer Tony Newman doing this years before and it sounded like great fun. I had visited a fishing shop a few days earlier, and had got a length of fishing line and some small hooks. I had made up some "lines" earlier (a short length of line with a hook at each end) and as I was talking to people, I craftily stuck a hook into their clothes, and then slipped away, repeating the process with a new target. Finally, I retired to a safe distance to watch.

People were amazed to see their clothes being pulled away from them, with the same thing happening to someone opposite. Clive Burr and Dave Potts were also in on the joke and were in tears of laughter, as the victims attempted to free themselves, whilst wondering what on earth was going on. A great laugh, but when they found out that I was the guilty party, I had to hide away once again until things calmed down. The fun quotient, as I remember, was far more enjoyable than the gig that night.

> **IRON MAIDEN** have switched their Portsmouth Locarno date from June 3 to July 1 and have added an extra date to their forthcoming tour at Norwich St Andrew's Hall on June 24.

Wednesday 28th May: Civic Hall, Wolverhampton
Another visit to this rain-grey town. I thought that Carlisle was the arsehole of England but it is not, Wolverhampton is. A totally forgettable night with an apathetic crowd. I don't know why all these people pay money to come and not have fun. Both bands played really well, and considering the paying public were supposed to be fans, I just couldn't put my finger on what went wrong that night. Steve Harris was not at all happy with the crowd's response to Maiden. Good job we all got hammered afterwards, and once again Di'Anno excelled himself by throwing the insides of sandwiches at the walls of the dressing room to see what would stick. And guess who joined in? Clive Burr, and, as you might have guessed... all started by me!

Thursday 29th May: Victoria Hall, Hanley
As we all arrived early, everybody (bands, roadies, lighting crew, uncle Tom Cobbly an' all) descended on the hotel that had been booked for us. An unbelievable situation was about to unfold. We had all been booked into an OAP centre!

The biddy on reception was visibly horrified to see us (young, long haired and fancily dressed) crowding into reception and tried to throw us out. Now we would all gladly have gone, but we were desperate for somewhere to stay, being absolutely knackered, with the late nights and the long days, so we refused to budge. They herded us into a back room (so that no other OAPs saw us), while Bob Adcock and Adrian (Maiden's Tour Manager) argued that, as we had booked in advance, then we were going to bloody well stay there. They finally relented but we had to agree to go into breakfast earlier than normal (which was a real pain in the arse) so that none of the old fogies saw us. When we left in the morning, I made a point of writing in the visitors book (you know, where polite people write, "a most pleasant stay, must come again" and all that shit, and in my very best handwriting I wrote, "a most terrible, horrid place. Shan't come again." All the chaps thought this was a brilliant wheeze and were 'hee-hawing' about it for most of the day.

The gig incidentally, was divinely average for both bands. It was not particularly well attended and the hall itself was cavernous (been there before) so the reverb was terrible, it was like trying to gig in the Grand Canyon. You have to bear in mind that, although Maiden were 'on their way up', it wasn't always a guarantee for a great gig.

On the way to the next venue, we had to travel through the Pennines (Britain's answer to a mountain range), by way of "Snake Pass". Now this may sound like a place in a western, but it is actually a very dangerous winding road and there are some hair-raising drops along the route. Cue: Bob Adcock. He loved a challenge, did Bob. He drove the "Hot Dog Van" as if it were a formula one racing car; he literally had it up on two wheels going through some of the bends. We were terrified, but the more we begged him to slow down, the more fanatically he drove. There was a back door in this excuse for a vehicle and I seriously considered jumping out of it a number of times during this experience, because I was utterly convinced that we were going to disappear into a ravine, never to be seen again. When we got though this accursed journey, the sense of relief was totally overwhelming.

Friday 30th May: Brunel Rooms, Swindon

A funny thing happened on the way to this gig. We were on the outskirts of the town, and whilst chugging down a long straight road, we passed a loan figure walking. I did a double take, for I recognised this strange person. It was none other than my old mate and ex-band member Pete 'Pierre' Sturgeon! Stop the van! I yelled. 'What the fuck?' The others shouted back, but Adcock, in complete obedience, braked so hard that the van almost stood on it's nose. I leapt out of the back door and we both ran towards each other shouting, "what the hell are you doing here?" He had apparently heard that we were playing in Swindon that night and had decided to hitch hike from his home in Milton Keynes (a considerable distance) to surprise me. He climbed in and I introduced him to the chaps. He had them all in tears of laughter with his stories of us in Germany, when we were both playing in Gypsy Love in '76 (don't mention the war).

The gig itself was great for both bands, but to be honest, unless something outrageous happened on the night, a lot of gigs blurred into one another. We would walk on stage, walk off to riotous applause an hour later and be on autopilot throughout the set. We had become like a well-oiled machine. I do remember that this place was actually a disco and it had a metal floor, which was great for sliding about on and precious little else. Some of the clientele were rather dubious. Michael Kenny, the PA mixer guy, kept being harassed at the desk and Bob and Vic (Maiden's minder) plus other members of the road crew, had to come to his rescue.

After the gig, all of us except for the Maidens (who had an up-market hotel) went back to our dive and sat noisily drinking in the bar. The manager, who quite clearly wanted to go to bed, came over and stated quite firmly that he was shutting, and would we all please piss off, which we did. Before too long, someone in our crew decided that he wasn't at all tired, and decided to have a game of "knock down ginger". As I am sure you know, this is a game where you knock on someone's door and run away. It can be hilarious, especially when played in your underpants! The mirth was finally halted, when both Tino and I where hammering on what we thought was Neal Kay's door, however, to our total surprise, it belonged to an elderly lady who screamed for her husband. We really didn't expect that... whoops!

Saturday 31st May: Cornwell Coliseum, St Austell

This was the furthest West we were to travel, and I was especially looking forward to it, because my ladylove Melinda was coming, along with a mini bus of her mates from Newquay, where she was doing a summer season. Bearing in mind we hadn't seen each other since the beginning of the month.

During the afternoon, we had loads of time to kill (as usual) so off went the rest of the chaps for a game of football. I went for a walk along the beach, and to my delight found an old hulk of a ship to explore (being a bit of a ship wreck anorak).

Back to the gig... I had looked round the hall before we went on hoping to see Melinda and her crew but no luck. As we walked on, I saw her waving from the back which put me on a big high, and I played the gig like a fucking demon. We finished the set to a wall of cheering and screaming. Bob Adcock, ever the old pro, had booked the missus and I into a hotel locally (without even having to be asked). A perfect way to end a perfect gig.

Needless to say, I didn't hang around for Maiden's set but I heard they played a blinder.

Sunday 1st June: Locarno, Bristol

After saying goodbye, we set sail for Bristol. The Locarno struck me as the wrong sort of venue for a metal gig, but then again a lot of the other venues were far from ideal (remember Grimsby on the first tour?) No one was, as I remember, particularly in the mood for playing that night, (both bands included). I do believe Messrs Di'Anno and Burr were in a highly mischievous mood. To make matters worse, I suggested that today's form of stupidity should once again revolve around the "hooking technique" and set about mingling amongst the various roadies, lighting crew and general throng of people. It was hilarious watching these poor sods wondering why their clothes were being pulled away, and turning round to see themselves hooked to some other unsuspecting fool, who was in turn, hooked to them. Getting a tiny fishhook out of your T-shirt whilst everyone else is pushing past you is no mean feat (I know because the bastards actually did it to me and Neal Kay) but it did feed our childish sense of humour.

The gig was okay, up until my pedal board decided not to work halfway through 'Captured City' and in a state of utter petulance; I kicked it hard across the stage, which did it no good at all. After the song was finished, our well-qualified roadies, Kenny Smith and Pete Bennett, came scampering onto the stage and before Tino had finished bullshitting the audience (to buy time of course) they scurried into the backstage darkness and all was sorted.

I did hear a legend that back in the early seventies in the true tradition of the "the gig must go on," that Kenny once repaired a Marshall amp head whilst the guitarist was actually playing a solo and kept the whole thing going. Fucking top men, both of them.

Monday 2nd June: Winter Gardens, Malvern

The trip to Malvern from Bristol was a fairly short one, so Herr Adcock took a good look round to find us a nice place to stay. Now Malvern is very sedate and middle class (Christ knows why this place was chosen for a metal venue). The hotel he chose was exactly the same. We were getting some piercing looks from the management as we were getting our bags in and there was more to come.

We had been there about half an hour, unpacked and were having a bit of a lay down, when Adcock decided to take a shower. As the rooms were not 'en suite', you had to use the single shower room, as did all the other guests. Within minutes we could hear a deafening tirade of obscenities coming from the aforementioned place. Almost instantly, the good lady proprietor came sprinting down the corridor and tearing open the shower room door, was confronted with a naked and very wet Bob Adcock, complaining in the most profuse language that the temperature was stuck on full heat and that his arse had been scalded! That was it. This woman totally lost it. She did no more than call the police! The more he tried to apologise the more adamant she became. Twenty minutes later in walked Mr Plod, complete with helmet under arm. When we heard him come into the hallway, we all assembled on the first floor landing (hidden of course) to hear the outcome. The lady hotelier insisted the he be arrested for swearing in a respectable establishment, but the wily Adcock completely played down the incident and after about half an hour of heavy duty wrangling, she actually apologised (we couldn't work out why). Mr Plod duly toddled out — after all there was no case to answer. Once again it proved the Adcock's powers of utter bullshit were at barrister level.

The gig: When we got there I couldn't believe that there were kids queuing hours before the doors opened. I have no idea where they all came from, as I said a place as remote and err... "un rock 'n' roll" as Malvern seemed like the unlikeliest venue for success, but gawd bless 'em, they were here ready and waiting. It was still light outside when we went on and someone had not pulled the blinds down. As you will be aware, if you ain't got darkness and stage lighting, half the mood is missing, (that's why I particularly hate doing outdoor gigs in daylight). The first three or four numbers took some getting into but after that we were sailing. Maiden's set was very well received that night with Di'Anno whipping the crowd up and taunting them, they loved it. Another town conquered.

Wednesday 4th June: Top Rank, Cardiff

As we had a day off before this gig Bob decided that we should all go to Barry Island for a swim. The sea was bloody freezing and the beach was just a load of rocks covered in seaweed. The only other thing of interest was the giant scrap yard where all the old steam locomotives were taken before being dismantled. For anyone with a sense of history, or a fascination with railways, it had an air of awesome dereliction.

Back to the plot: After the sound check degenerated into a shouting match between Di'Anno, Burr and the rest of the world, we all went to the local beach, which was only a couple of minutes away. It wasn't long before sand, dirt and all manner of flotsam and jetsam were being thrown and strangers were being splashed and generally soaked.

Back in the dressing rooms, the promoter had laid on beer and sandwiches (please note these big outrageous 'riders' in contracts, that now state such things as: Persian carpets, 25 gallons of champagne, three tons of caviar, two gross of blue smarties etc, being supplied before the band will even deign to sound check, had not yet been invented, so if you got beer and sarnies, you were doing alright mate).

This was to Messrs. Di'Anno, Burr and myself, an open invitation for a bun fight. Within minutes, the walls were splattered, along with everybody else with just about everything. No sandwich survived. Most beers were shaken (not stirred), then sprayed at all and sundry. I think both band's stage clothes were covered in beer and slime, but what the hell, its rock 'n' roll. I'm sure the audience must have noticed the cream buns in the hair and the odd bit of cucumber on the lycra trousers but who cares, we all had a great gig.

Friday 6th June: West Runton Pavilion, Cromer

The journey from Cardiff to Cromer on the East Coast is quite a long punch (as they say). When we all assembled there, the level of lethargy was amazing. We were well and truly knackered from the road. The sound check was just too much effort for all concerned. When it was over (quickly even by our standards), we stumbled out of the venue and found a nearby bar, with a veranda overlooking the sea. How very quaint. At least it was until the Di'Anno, Burr and Stratton squad toddled in. "Get them in Paul" I yelled across the bar. "Bollocks, you get them in" came the obvious reply. Heads turned in every direction and I think that the locals were somewhat perturbed. Once all the drinks had been bought, the Maiden contingent invaded our table and the inter-band banter (and abuse) began. It wasn't until we all promised to the management of this establishment most fervently, that we would lower their voices (and stop swearing) that we were all allowed to stay.

The gig however, was on a very low stage, barely eighteen inches high. It was difficult to see much past the front row, and the audience were to say the least, dangerously close. The security chaps had to pull over-enthusiastic fans off stage many times. On one occasion, some bloke got hold of the head of my guitar and wouldn't let go. I had to virtually tear it out of his hands and I thought there was going to be a bit of an 'incident', because he had a wild look on his face and definitely did not want to let go. When we started the next number, the guitar was about seventeen yards out of tune. I had to spend the rest of the song re-tuning the bloody thing (we did not have electronic tuners in those days). However, in the end a good night was had by both bands. I also have to say that during Maiden's set, Paul was taking full advantage of the proximity of the crowd, and mercilessly teasing them. This led to things getting very unstable at times.

I also seem to remember a bit of fracas in the lobby in the morning, when we were checking out of the hotel. The staff must have been totally relieved to see us go.

Saturday 7th June: Odeon, Birmingham

One of the most serious wheezes took place on this day. After the sound check, both bands and various members of the entourage left the venue by the front doors. Someone just happened to look up at the front of the building, where the panel showing the artist's names was displayed, and in letters about ten feet high, it said "RON MAIDEN" as if it was a single bloke performing. That was it, within seconds, everyone was rolling about on the pavement, howling with laughter. Everyone that is except the man himself — Rod Smallwood. He was absolutely fucking livid — he was seriously not amused. The band thought it was too brilliant for words, but no, Rod was going to sue somebody. Anybody. The management, the caretaker, the usherettes, somebody had be guilty and justice must be done! Eventually (after about a month) he did see the funny side of it... but it better not bloody well happen again.

The gig, once again, was brilliant for both bands, our on-stage sound was as near perfect as I had heard so far on the tour. An old mate of mine from school (who had played bass in my first band) came up out of the crowd and said hello. I hadn't seen him in years and I didn't know he lived anywhere near Birmingham. He had a big fancy looking camera round his neck and he was snapping away like David Bailey. And although loads of promises were made, I never did see those pictures.

Sunday 8th June: Top Rank, Sheffield
This gig was on a Sunday and I really fancied a good Sunday roast, instead of the usual motorway cafe garbage. Unfortunately, the gaff that we pulled into for lunch en route was a grimy, run down dump, in the days before motorway services were sanitised, globalised & whatever. You can imagine that a roast was definitely not available.

The "waitresses" in this joint had obviously taken a dislike to us and their attitude was quite frankly... fucking rude. However, a few beautifully acidic remarks from Mr Adcock took the wind from their sails, and when Tino called the one with spots "pus face"... well the poor cow did have a face resembling a currant bun, the hostilities really began. When this stroppy bird said, "I've 'ad enough of you lot, d'you want me to call the manager?" I replied, "Not if he's as fucking ugly as you are!" which brought hoots of laughter from the chaps. I do not remember a tip being proffered, but I do remember helping to top up the condiments with vinegar, and the sugar bowl by scraping soap into it just for a laugh.

At the venue, we all had to endure Maiden hammering away at full volume again in a near empty hall and wondering why no one in the band could hear the monitors.

I was in the 'dressing room' after the sound check (I use the term dressing room loosely), it was like a medieval prison cell and a certain person was prowling around as if he owned the place. He wasn't a member of either band... yet. It was none other than Bruce Dickinson. Makes you think doesn't it. I am sure Paul didn't see that one coming.

After the gig, which due to a poor turnout that night, finished remarkably on time, we all hit the booze and grub in the dressing rooms. From what I remember, Mr Dickinson joined in the fun.

Monday 9th June: Royal Court, Liverpool

Now, as this was Bob Adcock's hometown, we all had to promise to be on our best behaviour and play like we had never played before. No excuses.

With the sound check over, it was playtime. With a place like Liverpool, teeming with rock history, I demanded that Bob show us around. The site of the legendary Cavern Club had been bulldozed and renovated but various other lands marks were there. He made a special trip to show us the house where Ringo Starr lived as a kid. The others were not nearly as interested as I was, so they slid off to do other things, (play football?) while Mr Adcock told me about the heady nights at the Cavern at the height of the beat boom in the 'sixties. After all, if anyone should know, he should, because his rock career started as a roadie for the Mersey Beats a fairly successful band, who as far as I know are still touring today almost forty years later.

The gig went well, except for the foot monitors not working. This threw us, because when you feature three part harmony vocals, you really need to hear each other, although we got a great reception at the end, and they were yelling for more as we left the stage. There was no encore as we had overrun by around a ten minutes.

Maiden were also really on form that night and when they came off, I said to Den Stratton "could you hear the monitors?" He looked at me in complete surprise and said, "you must be fucking joking mate... at the volume we play, my ears have gone after the first five minutes and I am on auto pilot most of the time!" Fuck that I thought.

After the gig we were all raring to go out somewhere. Someone had heard of a heavy metal disco not far away, so obviously being complete gluttons for punishment, we set off to find the place.

Not being snotty, or elitist (moi?) we found it to be a bit youth clubbish, although the music they played was good (not that Neal Kay would agree), the most entertaining factor was the 'cabaret' ... a bunch of teenage bikers were doing a ridiculous dance (in formation would you believe) called... (prepare yourself) The 'Wanky Duck'! We stood there watching in complete amazement. This dance was indescribably absurd. It wasn't long before we were all in tears of disbelieving laughter, certain members of the Maiden crew attempted to have a go (Paul and Clive of course) but failed miserably, it was best left to these local kids. If only camcorders were available in those days.

Tuesday 10th June: Day off!

We had been given a day off for good behaviour and we were all wondering what to do. Bob Adcock has his usual brainwave, "Blackpool Fun Fair." Brilliant, pure genius. Off we went in convoy. I don't know what the normal people thought of us lot with long hair and fancy dress, turning up en-masse, but there was obviously an air of extreme mischief afoot.

As soon as we got in, the first ride was the Big Dipper. Now I have seen Big Dippers before at fun fairs, but this must have been used to train Stuka Pilots. I know my limitations, and there was absolutely no way I was going to have a go.

The rest of the tribe were as usual full of shit and rearing to go, especially 'you know who' from the Maiden camp. On they got, all shouting and hollering and showing off as the train of cars clanked into life. I stood there watching smugly from the sidelines.

Five or so minutes later, as the ride ground to a halt, the silence was deafening. All those loudmouths (I needn't say who) crawled out of the carriages speechless. Some being violently sick on the floor, others were green, and completely devoid of the usual bravado. That will fucking teach you cocky bastards, I thought, sniggering to myself.

Another toy to play with was the 'automatic arm wrestling machine'. The plan was to set the machine to maximum strength and get as many of us against it as possible. Even with Pete Bennett using both hands we still couldn't beat it.

The next stunt was the Dancing Horses — like a carousel that goes round and round, and the horses go up and down. When twenty or so blokes get on one of these, it is a recipe for disaster. After about the third go the bloke in charge decided that because of the high jinks and total disregard for safety, that we should all get off, but because of our sheer number he didn't like to enforce it too much. However we soon got bored and it was time for something else.

Meanwhile, Clive Burr and I had found one of those "laughing clown machines". As I am sure you all know, these things are really for children, because all that happens is you put your 10p in the slot (as it was then) and the clown in the glass cage wiggles about, pulling stupid faces, and a silly mechanical laugh comes out.

After the fourth go, I am bored... but Clive is seriously

impressed with this. I tell him I'm off and that I will see him later...

Half an hour or so later, I come back to find him lying on the floor, sobbing with laughter, unable to speak, then more of our mob arrive and are laughing at him. He had to be led away for his own good.

Later on in the afternoon, after we had all had a nice greasy burger, Bob Adcock demanded that we all went on this new scary ride called the 'Revolution'.

By today's standards, this ride would be pretty tame, but it was 'state of the (scariest) art' at the time. The ride consisted of being plunged into a complete 'loop the loop', which was gut wrenching enough, but what was worse; when you got to the end, it did the whole thing again backwards. Bloody good job we were harnessed in. I can't remember who was or wasn't sick, but I am sure a few of us had to lie on the ground for a few minutes to recover afterwards.

The next stop was the shop that sold jokes and novelties. It also sold certain risqué items and Clive chose a pair of crotchless knickers. You guessed it, the first thing he did after he had paid for them, was to pull them on over his head, where they stayed for the next couple of days with his tongue constantly poking out of the crotch hole. Ordinary citizens were most alarmed but the rest of us found it highly comical of course. He even wanted to do the next gig in this attire but I'm sure you can guess who said no way.

At the end on the day everyone had a great laugh and let off steam. We were more than halfway through the tour, but already the pressure was beginning to show. Various members of the road crew had fallen by the wayside (through lack of sleep and sheer exhaustion) and new faces were appearing to replace them. In both Maiden and ourselves, tensions were beginning to show, when you have got someone in your face 24/7 however much you get on with each other, chinks do appear in the armour.

Neal Kay, our resident DJ and "Master of Ceremonies", was starting to annoy the road crew. I like the bloke, but along with all us rockers, he had an ego visible from the moon. The chaps were beginning to think of ways to, let's say, 'take the wind out of his sails'...

Wednesday 11th June: Mecca, Sunderland

There we all were at the sound check, bored to tears, while Maiden hammered away to an empty hall getting the band sound level right. Now it was time for the vocal sound check. Come in Mr Di'Anno. I said come in Mr Di'Anno. Paul had gone AWOL. He was officially put on the missing list. No one had a clue where he was and roadies were sent in every direction to find him. After about an hour he swaggered in and everyone (especially Steve Harris) tore into him verbally. "wassa fucking matter wi' you lot then, eh – I only went for a piss, didn't I!" "Paul it doesn't take an elephant two hours to have a piss... now get on that fucking stage!"

Because of this incident, our sound check time was reduced to all of five minutes. Wow... thanks chaps.

The gig was just another case of going through the motions... the crowd had only really come to see Maiden, and despite our efforts on the whole, treated Mantis with a deafening wall of apathy.

After the gig, we went into Maiden's dressing room and the beer began to flow. I was personally feeling a little belligerent, because we had played our tits off to these tossers, who really weren't interested in us. Within minutes, beer was being sprayed around the place and sandwiches were smeared on walls. Before long the dressing room was trashed. I wonder who started it?

> **Praying Mantis**
> Sunderland
>
> I REALISE, of course, that giving a heavy metal band my nod of approval is a kiss of death tantamount to Mary Whitehouse endorsing the latest skinflick. But, it must be said, I thought Praying Mantis were all right.
> They've got an obliquely American persona to them, glossy and smooth with the Aerosmith/Angel pretty/ugly boy look. Like those bands Mantis lean more towards the hard rock than the out and out heavy and do it with a shade more class than your average third generation riff-riflers can generally muster. The vocals of the Troy brothers, guitarist Tino Iso that's what he's been doing since *Stingray* came off! bassist Chris and lead guitarist Angelo are excellent. There's nothing like lugging a band who can really sing and Mantis most certainly fit the bill. 'High Roller' has a great acapella section and the old vox expertise also gets the chance to sparkle on 'Lovers To the Grave'.
> Once attuned to what Mantis are about they do get a little predictable (show me a metaller who doesn't). Their songs, while some distance from crashing macho monotony do fall into clicheville when it comes to subject matter. And like seemingly every other HM band these days Mantis have written a song about themselves. A bit overplayed this one. Still, to play the game you've got to use the house's dice, I suppose.
> Mantis are well able to powerhouse along but have more on show than assault and battery of the earlobes. File under HM. For Mantis Music, rather than Metallic Mayhem (or *Melody Maker*).
> IAN RAVENDALE

Thursday 12th June: Caird Hall, Dundee

We had big trouble finding this for some reason and Bob Adcock was in a vile mood. He was doing his favourite trick of stopping to ask someone the way and if they stopped to think for more than five seconds, he would just roar away, causing much mirth with us chaps.

We eventually got there, and had the worse sound check to date; we played and sounded like amateurs. I don't know why but we just did. I got off that stage and thought to myself "what the hell has happened to us?" Adcock said not to dwell on it, let's just go and eat, and typical of him he knew a nice restaurant not far away.

After a well tasty meal and a few beers, we were in a far better mood. When we got back to the venue, it was packed. We went on and played one of the best gigs on the tour. The roar after we had finished hurt my ears. I believe there is an old adage:- lousy sound check, good gig and tonight that old saying was spot bollock on.

Friday 13th June: Apollo, Glasgow

After the sound check (which was much better than the previous night) the chaps took off to find somewhere to play football, in Glasgow... were they mad? I however, went trawling round the shops in the centre of town, and luckily found a second hand record shop. However, after a lot of anticipation, there was nothing that really caught my eye.

The Glasgow Apollo was a legendary venue in the early seventies (I can't quite remember why, but I am sure it was something to do with the amount of fighting that went on in the audience whilst the bands were playing) and it's stage was abnormally high, about ten feet (obviously to protect them from the regular affrays in the audience) and the whole place was covered in red glitter! Only the carpets (which were black with dirt, and trodden in chewing gum) and the windows were not glittered.

The gig itself went without a hitch (or a fight) but I didn't do my usual trick of running up the monitors, because if I had overbalanced I would have fallen and ended up in great heap at the foot of the stage.

We didn't stay for Maiden's set; we just went back to the hotel for a drink and called it a night.

Saturday 14th June: Town Hall, Middlesbrough

We were booked into a nice hotel here, and whilst having an early evening drink at the bar, we met a punky sort of band who were also playing somewhere in the town, called Pink Military. I am amazed that there were allowed into the place because of their clothes and general image. They made us lot look pretty normal.

When we were lurking about in the hall before the gig started, we met Janick Gers, who at the time was playing guitar in White Spirit, who if you remember, supported us at the Music Machine in Camden Town back in March. As I am sure you all know, Janick has been a member of Iron Maiden now for over thirty years.

Funnily enough, I didn't write an account of this gig at the time (I don't know why) so I assume it was neither terrible, nor special.

To me, the most interesting thing about Middlesborough, is that it is the birthplace of Paul Rodgers (Free, Bad Company, Queen et al)

Sunday 15th June: Unity Hall, Wakefield

Our first gig at the Unity Hall, on the Metal For Muthas Tour was a good 'un, so we hoped to repeat it. Maiden's sound check was even longer than usual, which gave us the right hump. When we eventually got on stage to do ours, someone yelled from the back of the hall "make it quick... the doors open in less than five minutes". Nice one chaps. We hurriedly played one song, but that was enough, we got the balance, and that was all we needed. Off we trundled, as Neal Kay was giving his usual opening speech, and barely had time to change before we were being announced. The crowd were absolutely roaring, we could do no wrong, and there was a constant sea of hands in the air. I was teasing them as I always did, by sweeping the guitar neck across the tips of their fingers, as if I was "machine gunning," and on a couple of occasions, someone jumped up and grabbed the head of my Les Paul. I had to wrench it out of their hands before I got pulled into the crowd.

At one point whilst "machine gunning," some bugger caught hold of the tuning peg of the B string and put the guitar well out. I had to finish the number trying to avoid playing the B string, which is pretty hard to do. The rest of the band were wincing as I was hitting bum notes, but when the number finished, and after a quick re-tune, we were ready to go again. Magically, the crowd didn't seem to notice. Thank Christ for that. Afterwards, I made damn sure not to swing the guitar too low over their grasping little paws. We finished the set to a deafening roar, but we were warned by certain parties not to do an encore, because, as at all rock gigs things were running "behind".

From the dressing room, we could hear Maiden's sonic assault, and I thought, how
can they play that loud? It's bloody painful.

On the subject of Maiden's volume level, I know that they all had trouble hearing the vocals from the monitors. Clive had monstrous "side fills" — large vertically mounted monitor speakers either side of him, pumping out hundreds of watts of sound, but he still claimed that he could only hear the guitars and the bass, whose amps were a good few feet away from him. I always thought that Mantis must have sounded feeble in comparison to Maiden, but a good few of the soundmen and crew assured me that we didn't. They said we had a different sound entirely to Maiden. It wasn't as heavy but it had more quality. They said that the strength of our songs didn't need that degree of volume (no offence intended Maiden, these comments were made 'without prejudice'). We just let the PA soundmen do their job in controlling the out front volume.

We had the next day off and as I didn't record what we did, I can only assume that we caught up on some well-earned sleep.

Tuesday 17th June: De Montfort Hall, Leicester

This was another legendary venue that had been going for years. I couldn't begin to list all the great bands that had played there, and I felt privileged to be playing on this particular stage.

All through the sound check, my pedal board kept cutting out intermittently, but Kenny and Pete had it in bits and sorted it ready for the gig. My "pedal board" at the time was a very home made affair. It consisted of a Colour Sound Wah pedal, an MXR Phase 90, and a Carlsboro Echo pedal, with the mains power unit sandwiched between two layers of chipboard, and it was of course painted black. Some of the connections could have been better, but after the last dodgy phase, Kenny had taken it to bits and "professionalised it".

Back to the gig — we played an absolute blinder to a brilliant crowd and Tino was so overcome with the occasion, that he walked to the front of the stage to shake hands with the front row (as we often did on a good gig) — the next thing we know, he had dived head long into the crowd. I now believe this is call 'moshing'. I couldn't believe he had done it. He disappeared for at least a couple of minutes before the roadies waded in to recovered his body. We were sure that he was dead, but he had a great big smile on his face. His clothes were completely ragged, he looked like he had been playing rugby, "ain't fucking doing that again," he said, breaking into a laugh. I think they pulled out half of his hair, along with bits of his clothes, as souvenirs. Nonetheless, a great time was had by all.

Wednesday 18th June: Central Hall, Chatham

As we all gathered for the sound check there were signs of dissention in the ranks. Various members of the road crew were showing signs of exhaustion and morale was sliding a little. Paul Di'Anno was telling me that he had had enough and (he was constantly being bollocked by either Steve Harris or Rod for his behaviour) so he decided that we would go "shopping" of all things.

The gig was, after the previous night's total triumph a complete non-event, with Neal Kay getting totally on everyone's nerves by continuingly telling all the band how they should have done it etc. However, true to form, good old Bob Adcock shredded him with some good old vitriolic Scouse wit.

Thursday 19th June: Civic Hall, Guildford

The thing that surprised me most about this gig, was that while we were walking back into the hall, after feeding our faces somewhere nearby for another grim sound check, was the amount of fans that were queuing early. On no other gig on the tour had I noticed so many kids massing outside so early. A good sign, no doubt. One or two started virtually telling us what our favourite colours were and what we'd had for breakfast last Sunday — they knew more about us than we did. Talk about keen.

The gig, the grand opening number... there we were in total darkness with the great Neal Kay giving us the good build-up. Wham, I hit the first chord of 'Rich City Kids' and nothing. Not a sound — the whole fucking backline had gone dead. Beam us up Scotty for fuck sake. Tino, Chris and I all had the same feeling of total horror, while Kenny and Pete scrambled around behind us, frantically testing things by torchlight, the crowd was growing restless. Neal Kay grabbed me by the arm "talk to the crowd for fuck sake" he shouted. "Fuck off," I said. "Who do you think I am? Fucking Max Bygraves? What do I say?"

After a couple of minutes (that seemed like a lifetime) all was back to normal, I then sauntered up to the mic and said something like "my lords, ladies and jelly spoons, that was just to show you that we were actually playing live and normal service will resume as soon as possible and I hope you will find it in your hearts to forgive those responsible." To which I got a big laugh and a ripple of applause from the crowd.

One-chew-free-four I went and we launched into 'Rich City Kids' with a vengeance. The rest of the set was a blur; the gig went down a storm.

It's okay when you can redeem yourselves after a mishap like that, but while it is happening, you feel utterly helpless and exposed, a bit like a Lancaster bomber caught in a searchlight over Berlin. Afterwards, we all had a serious drinking session in a pub across the road. I didn't catch Maiden's set that night, so sorry, nothing to report.

Friday 20th June: Rainbow Theatre, London

This was it, the big one, The Rainbow. In its day (from '71-'82) this was one of the biggest, most prestigious gigs in London. It was originally the Finsbury Park Empire and in about '63, the Beatles played there on a package tour.

It began as a proper rock venue in '71, after many years of disuse and I saw Alice Cooper there in November '71 for 50p, on their first UK tour. I had also seen Santana and Bad Company there, in' 73. For me to actually play there myself was a dream come true.

We got damn near a perfect sound at the sound check and hoped that the gig would be as good sound wise. Back stage, at about 4:00 in the afternoon, a phone call came through for me. It was the band's lawyer. He wanted to talk to me about my management contract. I ask you, what a ridiculous time to ring up. I had him on the phone for about an hour, talking all this legal shit, and as you can imagine, I was not the least bit interested. I was just going "oh right, yeah, yeah, yeah, absolutely", while he prattled on. The reason I had to talk him was because I couldn't make the band meeting with him sometime previously because of a bus and tube strike. Talk about inconvenient.

Time for combat: The celebrated Neal Kay gave us the big build up as usual and onto the stage we strode, to a big cheer. We steamed into 'Rich City Kids' to a big roar. We had them right from the 'off'. When we got to 'Lovers To The Grave' that starts moody and a cappella (Christ that sounds musical doesn't it), a certain person appeared at the front of the stage. My old mate 'Pierre' Sturgeon. He had a wicked look of glee on his face. All the time I am trying to sing serious harmony, he was trying to distract me. Guess what the bastard did then? He produced a can of beer and shook it wildly and then proceeded to spray me with it. The utter bastard. I was soaked, but the worse thing was, my guitar was soaked, all over the strings and neck, the stickiness makes it nigh on impossible to play properly and I had to battle hard to get through the rest of the song. Kenny came running on with my spare guitar, and I quickly swapped over between songs. Mr Sturgeon was still at the front looking extremely pleased with his self.

We finished to a deafening roar, and strode off stage triumphant. Bob Adcock had a look of pride, and he patted us all on the back with a "fookin' well done lads". I slunk out into the stage front area and there was Sturgeon grinning from ear to ear. "Trust you, you rotten bastard." He just sniggered. Compared to some of the stunts that we got up to in Germany in '76, while we were in Gypsy Love, being sprayed with beer during a song was really quite trivial. I said I would come and find him later for the after gig party after Maiden had finished but he said he had to go and get his lift home.

Maiden did their set and brought the house down, it was a great night for both bands, a good homecoming.

At the backstage party afterwards, I must say that I have never seen so many 'liggers', most of whom I didn't know from Adam, and most of them were too cool to acknowledge anyone from the Mantis camp. However, we got well pissed with our crowd. At the end, Bob picked us all up off the floor and took us home. A great night had been had by one and all.

Saturday 21st June: Sports Centre, Bracknell

After the Rainbow gig, to me it felt like the rest of the tour was surplus to requirements, but of course it wasn't, although it seemed an anti climax.

This Bracknell Sports Centre was a glorified gymnasium, with a makeshift stage which appeared to be made of what looked like school desks. We went on early and there was no blackout over the windows, so we played in daylight, which kills the atmosphere (no fancy coloured lights for us).

We had a fantastic gig regardless and we went off stage and out into the corridor to screaming applause where we waited. The applause didn't die off, so Bob Adcock said, "go on give them another one!" Just a minute, where is Chris, our bass player? Yeah, where is Chris? We went back into the hall, only to find that he had fallen down in between the desks and he was lying on the floor, with his bass still around his neck, completely dazed and bewildered! We couldn't help laughing as we dragged him out, and the audience thought it was all part of the act. Poor old Chris was still seeing stars as we played the encore. I remember back in around '72 doing a gig at the Sirius Club in North London, when pretty well the same thing happened. The bass player disappeared off stage to everyone's dismay and seconds later, two hands appeared over the edge of the stage, as he pulled himself back on. The name of that band was the aforementioned Big Ladder Woman.

Clearly a band can't be in two places at once.
Don't believe everything you read in the press.

Sunday 22nd June: Brangwyn Hall, Swansea

It seemed a long slog to Swansea, but Bob Adcock's driving made the journey interesting to say the least. As I mentioned earlier, he had a Formula 1 racing license, and he thought he could drive "the hot dog van" like a racing car no matter what.

When we had done our dutiful sound check, everyone

seemed to leave the venue and congregate on the beach, which was just across the road. I couldn't believe how many of us ended up there just mucking about and splashing each other.

After we had played (a good gig but nothing exceptional) we decided to hit the road home as we had a day off the next day. I thought that I would take my spare guitar home to play it. The thing was, I forgot to tell Kenny and Pete that I was doing so.

After we had left at the end of the night, the gear was being packed up and they discovered that my Gibson Firebird was missing. The police were called and there was a terrible scene (so I heard) and of course the guitar could not be found. When I saw them next, by which time they had found out that I had taken it without telling them, and because of all the panic and the terrible scene the night before, the pair of them wanted to fucking lynch me. Once the dust had settled we all had good laugh.

Tuesday 24th June: St Andrew's Hall, Norwich

It rained non-stop all the way to Norwich and because the main part of the journey was on the old (non dual carriageway) A11, it was a painfully hard slog. When we got there, I thought they had all made a terrible mistake and gone to the wrong venue. This place was more like a Cathedral than a rock venue. It even had a crypt. I must admit, I liked the vibe of the place and hoped that the rain would stop and we would get a good turnout that night.

Because of the acoustics of the place (tons and tons or reverb) we thought we had better sound check at less volume than usual. The Maidens took no heed of the sea of natural reverb, and as usual, their sound check was done at hyper volume, which of course means everything louder than everything else.

When we had finished sound checking, the rain had

actually stopped (at bloody last) so I took off for a walk around the town. I found a second hand record shop and a few dodgy back street guitar shops. Lots of interesting stuff, but alas no Selmer Amps, so I didn't buy anything.

The gig itself was far better attended than I expected and the kids in the front row knew all of our songs and were singing along to them. Chris and Tino were looking at me in amazement at the way the crowd knew our stuff. We were obviously better known than we thought. At the end of our set, the noise of their cheering, and the sight of all those hands pushing through the front to try and shake ours, was wonderful. The Maidens set however was marred by their over loudness and Paul's sullen attitude, which you could see was irking Steve, but nonetheless the crowd loved them.

Wednesday 25th June: Day off!
We got dropped off in the early hours after the gig and I slept through to midday. Usually we would have to be up early to set sail for the next one, halfway across the country somewhere, but today meant a well deserved lay in.

In the afternoon, I tinkered around with my guitars and amps and in the evening, I went out with a couple of mates for a few beers, but before I left I phoned my beloved, who was way down in Newquay.

Thursday 26th June: Apollo, Manchester
Bob Adcock picked me up last at about midday, so I got another lay in. We went steaming up the M1 and straight into a traffic jam. Poor old Dave Potts was dying for a pee and eventually out of sheer necessity, because we couldn't stop on the motorway he tried to do it out of the nearside window of the van. But he couldn't because everyone was laughing and as much as he was really busting to go, he was unable. He then tried to do it into a bottle of all things. If you have

ever tried this, in a van that is moving, you will know how difficult this is, and by now, our laughter was at fever pitch. Tino was holding his belly and I was holding my face, because my cheeks ached with laughter. Dave just gave up in the end, and when we eventually stopped at Newport Pagnell services he leapt straight out of the hot dog van and pissed against the wheel arch, in front of all and sundry. When we told the Maiden mob about it, they were all in hysterics, especially Messrs Di'Anno and Burr who, after a couple of pints, were known to laugh at the wallpaper.

The Maidens were in a playful mood while the gear was being set up (there had been a delay for some reason) so a game of hide and seek seemed like a good idea. After lots of coin tossing, Chris Troy was the poor unfortunate who had to find everybody. He started to count to fifty and about nine of us scattered in all directions. I don't know where the others went, but I broke into a cleaner's cupboard and pulled the door shut behind me. I just sat there in the darkness sniggering to myself while I heard various members of our entourage running past. I must have been in there about half an hour when I heard Chris, Tino and Dave Potts outside, wondering where the bloody hell the rest of them were. I couldn't contain my laughter anymore — they heard me and clawed open the cupboard to find me hidden behind a collection of vacuum cleaners, biting my thumb off trying not to laugh. Got you, you bastard. Next minute, someone was bellowing down the corridor that it was time for Maiden's sound check. Game over. Time to exit the building for at least an hour and get some grub.

After all the greasy burgers and chips money could buy, we all marched back to the venue, hoping the Maidens had done their sound check. It was far from over as there were problems with the power. For some unknown reason, it would switch itself off at irregular intervals. Fantastic, this was just what we needed. Electricians had been sent for, but had not yet appeared. Time was running out. Finally at about

6:45pm two blokes appeared in old-fashioned overalls, with plumber's style tool bags, looking like something out of a 1950s B movie (Eric Sykes and Bernard Cribbins look-a-likes) and began scratching their heads and tutting. Everyone left them to their job, praying that they could fix the problem. At about 7:30 they announced that they indeed had. "You sure mate? Only we have got a big show tonight," said Pete Bennett with just maybe a little menace in his voice. "Oh yes lad, you see blah blah etc etc..." Alright mate we believe you, the next thing they had hopped into their van and were off.

We got about ten minutes of our sound check but that was all we needed. Everyone was on hot bricks when the main doors were opened and Neal Kay was playing Motörhead at mega watts. We all had our fingers crossed, so far so good.

When Neal announced us, the reaction was mediocre to say the least. We were a little taken aback, because normally we received a good cheer upon being introduced. We could see that we were going to have to work hard. After about the third number they started to warm up and when we got to 'High Roller' I overdid the clap along bit on the intro and got them all going (whether they liked it or not) the rest of the set got increasingly better and as we ran off stage at the end it was to a big cheer, we had conquered them.

We hung around to see the start of Maiden's set (only because Paul had promised us that "something was going off tonight") he had been in a stroppy mood lately, because the tour was taking its toll on a lot of people, especially us "sensitive artists". After a couple of songs, he started bantering with the audience and some idiot at the front started haranguing him — not a wise move.

Paul singled the bloke out and almost challenged him to a fight after the gig. I could the see the look on Steve Harris's face and Rod Smallwood was only few feet away from us in the wings. He was shaking he head in utter disbelief. I looked at Bob Adcock, and he said "fookin'ell lad... " and we slunk away before things turned nasty, obviously missing the rest of their set, we heard later that Paul's mood and attitude did not improve although they went down extremely well.

In the pub across the road, we were recounting the incident and Bob was telling us hair-raising tales of punch-ups and near riots in Liverpool, in the Merseybeat days. Apparently one on the main ingredients of being in a band in Liverpool in the early sixties was being handy in a fight. It was rite of passage that bands got picked on at gigs. I am glad things have calmed down since then, but even in my early days of playing at youth clubs and dance halls, I have seen some bloodbaths. On some occasions, bands had had all their gear and their vans smashed up, often for no apparent reason.

Friday 27th June: Pavilion, Bath

When we got to Bath, everyone was showing signs of "battle fatigue". We had been on tour constantly, with only a couple of days off here and there, for the best part of six weeks. Us pampered, poor little 'rock stars' only really have to play for about an hour a day and while we are travelling, we can sleep if we want, obviously because someone else is driving. Now the road crew and lighting boys have to spend hours and hours setting up the gear, making sure it works and if it doesn't making damn sure that they fix it. Also they are on duty while the bands are playing and then at the end of the night, take everything to pieces and load it into the trucks and then drive through the night to the next gig wherever that may be. These blokes deserve to be fucking knackered. A lot of them got to look like zombies, and tempers are lost at the slightest silly thing.

In the dressing room at Bath, I was fascinated to see all the graffiti. It had been a tradition for bands to "leave their mark" on the walls and every band who had ever played there had written their names somewhere, which for me being a rock and roll "anorak" made excellent reading.

The first "proper" gig I went to see, that is, not something at a local youth club was when I saw John Mayall's Bluesbrakers at the Cooks Ferry Inn in Edmonton, North London, in June 1968, when I had not long turned 16. The place was packed to the rafters and the atmosphere was electric. As a special treat that night, none other than Peter Green, John McVie and Mick Fleetwood, all from Fleetwood Mac were in the audience and John Mayall got them up on stage near the end, to provide a little "cabaret" which they did with relish, all being totally pissed. And the place exploded. All this for 5 bob (25p that is).

Ever since, I have been completely besotted by rock music and the whole package — the bands; who has played with who; guitars, amps, records, posters etc. I am sorry if I am digressing a little, but I thought I would just let you know what a complete and utter fan I am, and to play some of these venues on the tour, and realise and see who has gone before completely holds me in awe. Sad bastard eh?

Back to reality: The monitor at the front of the stage wouldn't work. To be honest, I don't think it mattered to Maiden, because their backline was so loud that not hearing the vocals became the norm. The difference with us was that we played a lot quieter than Maiden, and featured three part harmony vocals, so we needed to hear those vocals. I know that I certainly do, so I know when I am singing in tune.

It appeared that no matter what the sound tech tried, the slave amp that powered these front monitors was knackered and the only good news was that the side fills (vertically stacked monitors at the side of the main PA) facing inwards to the stage were okay. It made the onstage sound a little different but we had to live with it.

For some reason, we didn't get to the hotel before the gig, so obviously none of us got to have a bath or shower. We had to go on extremely grimy and we must have stunk, especially because our stage clothes were in need of a wash by now.

Once we were on stage, we quickly got used to the sound being different and by about the fourth song, we were well and truly in gear. The constant night after night gigging was making us well and truly tight and we sailed through the set, to growing applause from the crowd. They demanded an encore so we tore into 'Rich City Kids' again and I went right to the front of the stage for the clap along bit. As I did so, I felt what seemed like hundreds of hands grab at both my feet. I thought, "shit I am in trouble here." I couldn't move at all. I turned to my left and Pete Bennett was stood there, I pointed to my feet and he instantly read the situation. He came lurching on stage like Guy the Gorilla and started prising hands from around my feet and ankles. I turned and did a backwards skip and jump to get myself back to the mic, trying to make it look as theatrical and rehearsed as ever. We came off stage to a roar and in the wings I thanked Pete for saving me. "Part of the job mate," he said with a confident smirk on his face.

When Maiden came on stage, I could tell Paul was suffering from the lack of front monitors. He was naturally singing harder than usual because he obviously could not hear himself at all and he was sweating profusely. You could see the veins in his neck standing out. They still did a great set though and when they came off to tumultuous applause, I asked him if he had been struggling, to which he said "they better get them fucking monitors sorted for tomorrow or I am going AWOL!"

Let us pray

PRAYING MANTIS, currently on tour with Iron Maiden, have signed to Gem Records and have a single called appropriately 'Praying Mantis' released July 4.

The Mantis have recently changed drummers and now have Dave Potts, who was previously with Alvin Lee's Ten Years After reformation band.

Saturday 28th June: New Theatre, Oxford

When I got up that morning, I had a serious soak in the bath. It was heavenly. I felt like a new man. We all had a good scrub and a hearty breakfast, because the day before we hadn't had a chance to eat properly.

When we got to Oxford with plenty of time to spare, the others found a park to play football in, so I went off around the city looking for a record shop and hopefully a back street guitar shop. Unfortunately I found neither, but whilst in the local Woolworths (sounds familiar) I noticed two suspicious characters. Once again (I mention no names) I asked, "ain't you's supposed to be at the sound check? "Fucking sound check? What's the point, same old noise every night innit". Words of wisdom no less.

I left them to it and made my way back to the venue, only to find the rest of the Maidens looking frantically for them. I casually mentioned that I had seen them in a certain department store and Rod Smallwood turned on me and roared, "Woolworths, Woolworths, what the fuck are they doing in Woolworths?" I didn't quite know what to say, because by now, Rod Smallwood was so enraged that his face was like a gargoyle! He started barking orders at various members of the Maiden ensemble and sent some troops off to the town to collect the wayward pair at full speed.

Minutes later the angelic pair came nonchalantly toddling into the hall only to be greeted by Smallwood bellowing, "and where the fuck do you think you've been?" It was just like being back at school. Smallwood tore into both of them and within seconds, there were stood there, heads hung, just like naughty schoolboys. I couldn't let this moment escape. I sidled round behind Smallwood and waited until they both looked at me then I pulled a really cheesy face and that was it. They both had hysterics, which of course made Smallwood's anger intensify. By this time, nearly everyone else in the hall had turned to look at the fracas, and as Paul and Clive (and me of course) were sobbing with laughter, Smallwood strode off, his face as red as a beetroot, boiling with anger. Steve Harris walked up looking deadly serious and said "if I were you two I would get up on that fucking stage right now if you know what is good for you." Joke over chaps.

After we had all sound checked, there was still about an hour and a half to kill, so we all went over the road to a pub. Rod Smallwood was in there, sitting on his own, so we kept well away, as it was obvious that he was still extremely peeved. The two culprits were up at the bar, plucking up the courage to approach him, we were all watching in complete anticipation as they went up to him and said innocently, "...err, want a drink Rod?" Smallwood fixed them both with a real 'Clint Eastwood' gaze and said, "don't you two ever give me or the rest of the band any more shit or you will both be back on the fucking dole — understand?" "Err... yeah okay... sorry," they both replied," tails firmly between their legs. Smallwood then said, "now where is that fucking beer then eh?" I think the ice was beginning to melt.

While they were up at the bar, the celebrated Neal Kay came swaggering up to them "who's the naughty boys then," he said with glee. "Fuck off, hippy," was their reply, almost as if it had been rehearsed — another tail between another pair of legs.

The gig incidentally was crap for both bands. The audience must have been on tranquillisers that night. I don't think that any of us had ever witnessed such a disturbing case of acute apathy. I couldn't believe that these people had actually paid to see us and come with such an attitude. Paul came out with a classic at the end of the Maiden set... "now fuck off home and drink your fucking cocoa, you useless cunts!"

Sunday 29th June: Top Rank Brighton

This was the penultimate gig on the tour and most had had enough, with morale crumbling rapidly. Everyone wanted to go home to see their wives, girlfriends and families. The road crew had been racking their brains to think of a stunt to pull on poor, unsuspecting Neal Kay. Adcock came up with a classic. Neal's records were stored in boxes, which were locked and stowed away with all the gear in the trucks. The trick was to unscrew the locks, so that they could be opened and the records changed around into the wrong sleeves. They chose his favourite albums so it would work to maximum effect. When they had finished, the boxes were reassembled and the chaps could barely contain their mirth.

Just before show time, Neal was sorting all his favourite albums and getting them ready to play with the first one being ZZ Top. Luckily this one hadn't been tampered with. He started playing it as the crowd came in. He then announced a track by Molly Hatchet and alas in the sleeve was UFO or something. Poor Neal was totally baffled by this, as all boxes had been locked and stowed away. He was getting more and more frustrated as this process continued, and everyone was watching him (as we were all in on the joke). He eventually twigged it "you cunts, you fucking cunts," he screamed, which must have been picked up by the mic and that was it... the chaps were rolling on the floor in hysterics. Pete Bennett was laughing so much that he couldn't breathe and all of us in turn were laughing at him. After this, the ultimate humiliation, Neal would speak to no one except of course his "helpers", and these poor sods were also his whipping boys, who would undoubtedly bear the full force of his anger.

When it was time for us to go on, instead of the big build up we normally got, he barely mumbled the band's name so there was no sense of event. We did however, slay the crowd. We could have slayed them even more if the mics hadn't been live. Every time our mouths touched them, we got a mild electric shock which was extremely off putting. True to form it, hadn't happened in the sound check but it bloody well did on the gig. Maiden also suffered with it during their set, and I could see Paul wincing every now and then, as he was singing. When they come off (after a deafening encore) poor old Mike Kenny got a serious 'throating' from the Maiden hierarchy, even though it wasn't his fault. In situations such as this some poor fucker has to take the blame.

Tuesday 1st July: Locarno, Portsmouth

The day had at last arrived — the last gig of the tour. We, Praying Mantis that is, knew that something was being planned by the road crew to "enhance" our last performance. After the stunt they had pulled on Neal Kay the previous night, it was obvious that he was still extremely narked, because instead of being full of chat, he just kept himself quite whilst he sorted through his records to ensure they were where they should be. He did however, give us a good build up and announce to the crowd that as it was the last night of the tour, and that "anything could happen".

We went on to a rousing cheer and steamed into our set. When we got to the point where there were about two songs left, I took it upon myself to demand for a big round of applause for the "unsung heroes", the road crew, lighting crew, truck crew and tour managers etc. I told the crowd (in a speech that Henry V would have been proud of) that while the bands might make it rock, these blokes who are never really noticed by the audience in general, certainly made it roll, and do their jobs to a level far above and beyond the call of rock 'n' roll. A great resounding cheer rang out from the crowd and quite rightly so.

As we romped into the last song of our set, all of a horrible sudden, the stage began to fill with smoke. The bastards had begun to spring their "surprise" on us. Now this smoke got to a level where you couldn't see you hand in front of your face and various roadies armed with cans of spray string fought their way through the confusion to spray us constantly with the horrible stuff. It was damn near impossible to concentrate on playing while your instruments and your body are covered in it and the fact that the smoke was so thick, meant we were having trouble breathing. Dave Potts told us afterwards, that he was close to panicking and passing out. We finished the song to a deafening roar from the crowd, and just to be "theatrical" I kicked the mic and stand into the audience! Luckily no one was hurt. If I had done that sort of thing today I would of been sued, no doubt.

Back stage, all the crew members were patting me on the back, and saying thanks for the mention and what a speech. Bob Adcock held out his hand to shake mine and fixed me with a sincere look. "Nice one la', fookin nice one."

I felt honoured to have worked with these blokes, not just the old pros on our team, but everyone concerned with the tour. It might not have been like going to war, but the

camaraderie between the chaps was great, and they all pulled together beautifully under the pressure and duration of it all.

The sense of apprehension before Maiden came on was phenomenal. The crowd were chanting "Maiden, Maiden, Maiden" and as they took to the stage the screams of anticipation were quite painful. It must have been louder than Maiden actually played and that was saying something. They played a blinder that night and Paul was in amazing form. His rapport with the audience was absolutely inspiring. Each time they thought they had finished, the crowd just kept demanding more. I lost count of the encores they played and backstage afterwards the atmosphere was electric. Everyone was buzzing. A truly great end to a hard working tour. Both bands had invaluable exposure to the public and as our single ('Praying Mantis' b/w 'High Roller') was due out within days, we were hoping for good sales. And just recently Maiden had released 'Sanctuary' as a single and as far as we knew it had just got to number 27 in the top 30.

The after gig festivities were in full flow, but I had something in mind. I had a midnight train to catch, I was going home briefly and tomorrow I was catching the bus to Newquay in Cornwall.

I spent a week there with my Melinda and I had missed her an unbelievable amount whilst we had been away. I used to phone her at a phone box by Newquay railway station at 6:00 in the evening regularly.

And now, from London... Praying Mantis!

(Courtesy Freddie Silva)

Our single released in July 1980 to coincide with the tour. 'Praying Mantis' b/w 'High Roller'.

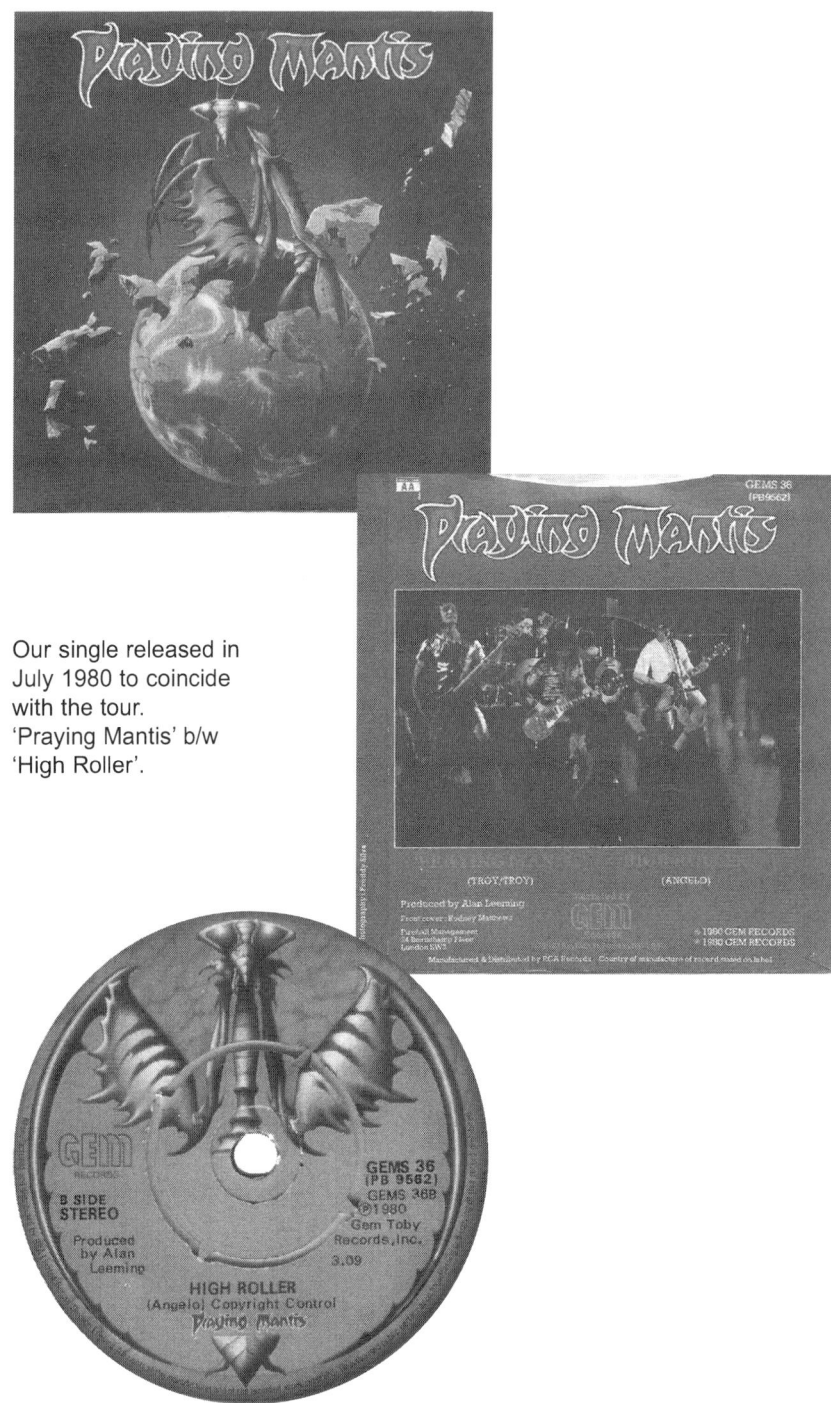

THE AFTERMATH —
A BOLT FROM THE BLUE

When I got back from Newquay, I phoned the management office to find out what was next on the agenda. I noticed a hesitant tone in the receptionist's voice, when she told me that I was to "come to the office next Tuesday at 1 o'clock". When I got there, I perceived an icy atmosphere and a total lack of the previous, friendliest manner that I was used to. The two managers sat me down and told me that the others in the band didn't want to continue playing with me. I was completely shocked. Gobsmacked. "Why, why exactly?" They explained that although I was good on stage, they felt that I wasn't a "team" player. They thought that my heart wasn't really in the band and that I was playing the "prima donna" too much. I didn't have a clue what to say. They had obviously made up their minds. I came out of that office in a state of utter bewilderment. The managers did tell me that if I was going to "get something of my own together", that I was still "under contract" and that they would "help me as much as they could". I was numb; I hadn't a clue what to do next. The feeling of ecstatic elation after the tour had gone. To be cast aside so brutally was incomprehensible. I just didn't have any idea what to do or how to come to terms with it.

After a few days of trying to get my head round it, I phoned GEM Records (a small subsidiary of the mighty

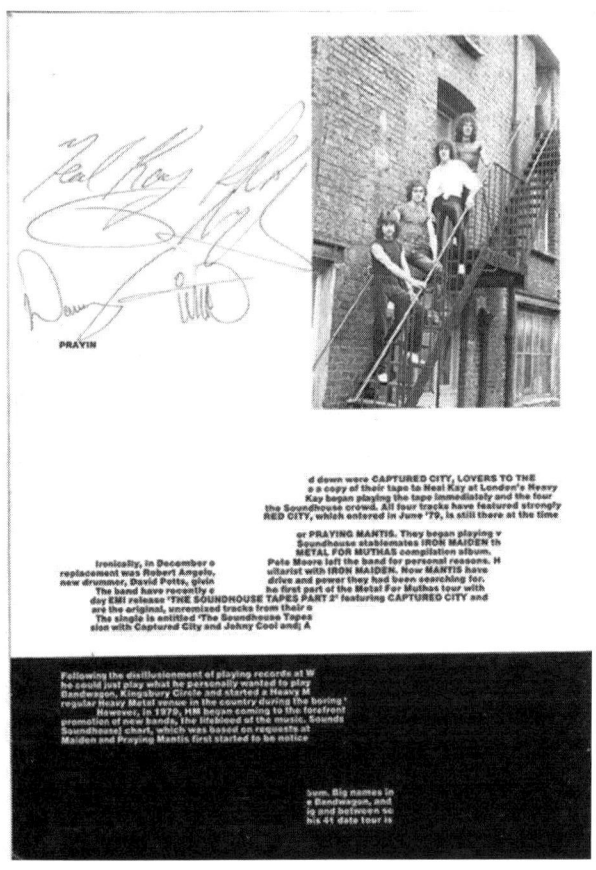

RCA) and they invited my down to their offices for a meeting. They had heard about my being fired from the band and because of it had decided to let Praying Mantis go. This made me feel far more valued but I was sad it had to end that way. They said that whatever I wanted to do, they would be behind me. I thought another period in Newquay was in order. Time to play "Rock Stars in Exile".

We came back from Newquay in September and straight away rang GEM to let them know of my return, and that I was ready for my next venture (whatever that may be). The reply from them was, "Rob who?" sorry, you were offered your chance a couple of months ago and you didn't take it, so good luck for the future. Christ what now? Talk about a double whammy I thought. I felt shattered before, but this was absolutely crushing. I didn't even want to touch my guitar at this point. I had absolutely no idea what I was going to do and no inspiration whatsoever. To make things even more painful, wherever I went, I would bump into people who knew me from the band, or even strangers who had seen Mantis play somewhere, and wanted my autograph. Talk about having you nose rubbed in it.

After a few months, my interest returned, and I wrote a

few songs. I phoned my "managers" and they helped me assemble a band with my old mate Ron Rebel. We went into a studio, and made a demo of four songs. My management couldn't be bothered to do anymore at this point, so I made an appointment with Double D Records, which was run by none other than Dave Dee, of the Dozy, Beaky, Mick and Tich fame. I played him the demo and I could see that he wasn't that impressed and he passed on it. I also got an appointment with Zomba Publishing, who looked after Maiden's material. I played them the demo, and they too were unimpressed. They heard no "hit records" which was pretty well what Dave Dee had said.

By this time I had completely lost faith in having a professional music career. I realised it was all too fickle and that there was no form of security in it whatsoever. I had learnt that, although Mantis were a big success on the tour, they had incurred a huge debt and the band themselves had barely seen any money (plenty of promises, but no money) so I developed a deep mistrust of the corporate side of rock. From now on I wanted nothing to do with it.

Months later, I was offered a place in a band playing the occasional pub gig by an old mate, and although it was really only a labour of love, I knew where I stood. Almost a year after my departure from Mantis, my old mate Danny Hynes rang me up; he wanted me to join his band Weapon. Months earlier, they had played support on a six week tour with Motörhead and finished at the Hammersmith Odeon for four nights. Well I thought, maybe its time to put my toe back into the water. I joined them in July 1981 alongside Baz, our old bass player from Snatch, Jeff Summers on guitar, and another new member, John Phillips on drums (ex-Lone Star).

Weapon had secured a publishing deal with Virgin Records. Virgin financed their demos at The Manor, a huge recording complex in Oxfordshire, owned by Richard Branson. The cruel irony was that, although Virgin gave them their publishing deal, for some unknown reason they wouldn't give them a record deal. We rehearsed and did a few London gigs and various A&R men came to see us, but with no result.

Our luck almost changed when we were approached by a big successful record producer to front a Status Quo medley that had been recorded by session men, and was getting near the Top Thirty. If it had of achieved a slot, then a Top of the Pops appearance would have been required. We rehearsed this medley, and were getting really excited (sad or what?) when it completely dropped out of the charts and that was the end of that. This record producer made it clear that he wasn't interested in our own material and had merely wanted us to front the medley if had been successful. Another dead end. The band struggled on for another couple of months and then slowly ground to a halt. I was still playing in my mate's pub band and after this I said to myself no more. I just couldn't take the disappointments. At least with a pub band you know where you stand.

Over the years, I have lost count of how many people who have said to me "I bet you wished you had never left Maiden" but it wasn't as straight forward as that. It has given me some distinction to have played with them and Praying Mantis, who were very much respected by their peers. The thing to bear in mind is that egos seem to run very high in rock bands, especially so in heavy metal bands for some unknown reason, maybe that is why metal bands change personnel so often.

I didn't see anything of Chris and Tino, or Dave for that matter, for a good couple of years or more but we are mates again now. Ironically, I was offered the job of guitarist in Paddy Goes To Holyhead by a certain Danny Hynes, who formed the band to play pubs (he too had had enough of professional rock and roll at the time) in March 1988. I would have been playing guitar alongside Tino and replacing Andy Scott (of the Sweet) who had decided to quit and return to the Sweet. The only way to describe how these band members intermingle is incestuous to put it mildly!

Den Stratton, previously with Maiden was at one time playing in Mantis and Bruce Bisland who replaced John Phillips in Weapon, is now drumming with The Sweet.

Since leaving Weapon, I have played with a few bands, but not in any professional capacity. In short... for the fun of it.

I still see on occasion, Ron Rebel, Dennis, and Terry Wapram from the Maidens, and Tino from Praying Mantis and recently bumped into Jeff Summers from Weapon: UK at a local gig.

With Ron Rebel at his place, summer 2015.
Ron was in Weapon for a while in 1983.
He also played with the late Paul Samson,
who I met at an audition in early '74,
and through Paul, I joined Moby Dick.
I told you this band lark was incestuous, didn't I?

Den and I around 2014.

What a bunch of old maidens.
Left to right: Barry Purkis, Tony Moore, Terry Rance, Me,
Dave Sullivan, Dennis Willcock, Terry Wapram, Doug Sampson.

POINTS OF TRIVIA

I still do the occasional gig and have recorded several albums of 'ambient musik' in my home studio but in the context of this book, I suppose that is fairly irrelevant.

I was lucky enough to see 'live' (back in the day) for what is now not even the price of a pint:
Led Zeppelin, Deep Purple, Black Sabbath, Free, Jethro Tull, Taste, Aerosmith, Alice Cooper, Ten Years After, Family, Steppenwolf, Queen, Santana, Bad Company, MC5 and countless others. And the best band was... Golden Earring!

I am naturally left-handed, but I play guitar right –handed.

I was once (in my 'normal' life) the telephone engineer for Eton College.

My first public appearance (sorry, 'gig') was at my school Christmas Concert, in 1964. We were called the Silent Flights. I played harmonica. We were shit, but it broke the ice.

One time Drummer in Highroller (late '83) was the late Steve Gadd who went on to be Drum roadie for Nicko of Iron Maiden.

The most famous musician I've ever played with was Ginger Baker from Cream. He was looking around for musicians to form a band with. The highlight of that evening was when his manager took us all for a Chinese meal afterwards.

I once supported my all-time hero Steve Marriott, at the Royal Standard, Walthamstow, back in '84. He did not disappoint and we talked for ages after the gig. He told me everything about the old days... all the 'rip-offs' and some.

Another hero I met, was Marc Bolan. What a seriously nice bloke. He didn't just have charisma, he fucking invented it.

My top 5 favourite rock) guitarists are:-

Leslie West
Michael Schenker
Jeff Beck
Jimi Hendrix
Eric Clapton
But not necessarily in that order.

I have, in the distant past, auditioned (unsuccessfully) for Supertramp, Love Affair, Edgar Broughton Band and Dr. Feelgood.

Although I have been in a few 'metal' bands, my favourite type of music is early 'seventies progressive rock, psychedelic and progressive jazz.

I believe that there was a story going about years ago years ago that I threw a vintage Les Paul across stage in a fit of anger. It was actually a Gibson Firebird 7 and when it hit the wall the head broke clean off. The audience gasped in amazement and I just picked up another one and carried on as if nothing had happened. I cried my fucking eyes out later that night. The Firebird was magically repaired by Dave Edwards (of the band RDB) and I played it for years after, until I eventually tired of it and I sold it to buy my first PRS Guitar.

For all the years I have spent playing I rarely ever saw any money but what the hell the fun content was immeasurable and the memories are priceless.

GUITAR TRIVIA

Whilst in Maiden I played a Gibson Les Paul 1968 Goldtop, which was originally fitted with P.90 type pickups. As soon as we started playing at the 'Cart, I began to experience serious noise problems. The P.90s would pick up the interference from the dimmers on the lighting desk, along with more noise caused by any neighbouring fluorescent lights. This problem actually gave me sleepless nights. I stripped the guitar down, and 'screened' all the electrical parts, but to no avail. There was only one real course of action. I had to change the pickups. This was not something I wanted to do, because it would certainly 'desecrate' an original Gibson guitar, but unfortunately, it had to be done. The only choice was, which pickups to buy? Gibson standard humbuckers were available in Britain at this time, but so also were Dimarzio replacement pickups, and as soon as I heard about them, I went straight up the West End and brought a pair. They were about £65 each, which at the time, was mega expensive — bearing in mind that I was only taking home about £40 per week from my job at the Ford Motor factory. However, as soon as I put the DiMarzio's on the guitar, it was like... Jesus! No hum! Instant wailing sustain — it turned my Les Paul into a monster and I was in tone heaven!

Anyway back to the plot...my spare guitar was an Antoria Flying V, an exact copy of the original Gibson 'Futurist' Flying V, but it wasn't a patch on the Les Paul sound wise.

My amp was a Master Volume Fender Twin Reverb, not a classic hard rock amp, but with the Les Paul it was dead right – I still have this guitar today, and it has undergone many transformations – it presently has a beautiful flame top, and the pickups have been changed (again...) to make it look, and sound like an original '59 Les Paul.

WHERE ARE THEY NOW?

Some of the musicians I've played with in the past, have gone on to greater things, some haven't. From Snatch: Danny Hynes and Baz Downes went on to form Weapon along with Jeff Summers. I was also in this band from July-November 1981. Weapon are currently riding high with a new CD album out, and doing big gigs. Drummer Darryl Read sadly was killed in a motorbike accident in Thailand in 2013. Prior to his death, we had loosely discussed forming a CREAM tribute band (of all things).

From Nitro: Dennis Willcock formed V.1 with Terry Wapram after their stint in Maiden. They both disappeared for years, but are now back with a new line-up of V.1, and are doing very well. Dennis was also in the band Gibraltar prior to the reformation of V.1.

Guitarist Alan Warner is now back with the Foundations (the band he started with, back in the sixties) and they play at sixties package shows, with many other bands from their period.

Drummer Vic Scott became a bit part actor and still plays in bands out in the depths of Essex.

Bass player Kevin O'Brien played in Joker and now lives somewhere near Huntingdon, and plays in a covers band called Red Sox.

Ron Rebel played with Bernie Tormé and ex-Gillan Bassist John McCoy back in the 1990s but has not played for a while due to ill health. We live about a twenty minute drive from each other, and socialise occasionally.

'Loopy' one of the 'Maiden Road crew from the tours, has written his own very informative book about the goings on during his period with Maiden. I hadn't seen him for thirty-eight years, until recently when my band Firebird Seven played at a Burrfest event, at none other than the good old Cart & Horses in Stratford. He was there and Loopy and I had a good old chinwag about the old days.

The only time that I have ever played in the same line up with Paul Di'Anno since the tour was in 1985 at the Royal Standard in Walthamstow, which was local to us both and a big rock venue. We had already played there regularly in our respective bands, him with Battlezone and me with High Roller and later Nitro Blues.

The first gig we did together was in February 1985, a midweek charity event to raise money for cancer research. I recall that by the time we both got on stage, we were very pissed. I remember Paul singing (acapella) Janis Joplin's 'Mercedez Benz' and all of us doing a calamitous version of 'Alright Now'.

I also remember the slide guitarist in the band, Graham Hynes (aka Terry Dactyl, who had a hit in 1972 with 'Seaside Shuffle') giving Paul and I seriously disapproving looks because of our cavalier performance. The rest of the night was a total blur. Christ knows what happened after that or how I got home.

The second time was on the same bill but in separate bands, again at the Royal Standard, this time in July 1987. It was a free concert to raise money for a scanner appeal for a local hospital. Nitro went on first, followed by various local bands, including Tilt, Tokyo Blade and Paul's band Battlezone. At the end of the night, various musicians got up for an almighty jam, with Paul and me leading the charge. I think 'Alright Now' was played again that evening!

With both our bands playing so regularly at the Standard, we were always drinking and ligging there and Paul was virtually in residence. However, typical of him, after a drunken argument one evening (so the story goes) sometime in early 1990, he was barred from his own "kingdom" and I haven't seen him to this day, which is a shame because we were both naughty boys together and had plenty of scrapes together, especially on the tours.

There was at one time (about mid 1986) talk of a local "super group" being formed. It was to consist of Paul, Tony Knightsbridge on bass (a local character who had a killer blues voice), possibly Ron Rebel on drums, and myself, but after a lot of rumours, it never happened.

Not long after I was fired from Maiden, they got a keyboard player in for short while called Tony Moore. I went to an audition in the depths of Kent in August 1979 and he was the keyboard player in the band. I hadn't met him until that day but after I had auditioned, we chatted, and realised that we have both been in Maiden. Talk about a small wood... sorry... world!

Out of all the bands and stars that I have met along the way, Nazareth were without doubt the friendliest. Earlier in the book I described the encounters when Mantis supported them and they were by far the warmest and most generous of all, gawd bless 'em.

The friendliest star (much to our surprise) as he was so famous, was Marc Bolan. I previously mentioned we met him in some rough pub on the wrong end of Kings Road Chelsea one Sunday lunchtime. I can't stress enough how enthusiastic and open he was and he and I were talking guitars for ages. As I said before, he didn't just have charisma — he fucking invented it. Great bloke sadly missed.

OTHER ENCOUNTERS

I have crossed paths with a few old faces and various bands from the sixties and seventies. In November 1970 my band at the time Big Ladder Woman (killer name, eh?) supported Hawkwind at the Sirius Club in Southgate, North London. They let us use their 200 watt Hiwatt PA as we didn't actually own one ourselves. Everything was fine, until halfway through the set, when they turned their strobe light on, which was facing directly at us from the balcony. This thing was as big as a World War Two searchlight and within an instant we were visually and mentally wiped. Slaughtered. We just couldn't continue. How they played their own set with this thing at full pelt in their eyes defies any form of logic, but they did, night after night for years!

I also auditioned, back in August 1971 for an obscure band called Supertramp. This was three years before their epic album *Crime of the Century*. Apparently 150 guitarists were auditioned at Cabin Studios, in Shepherds Bush, West London in a space of two days. In the end, the bass player, Roger Hodgson switched to lead guitar.

In May 1974, I did an audition with a band which consisted of ex-members of both Skin Alley and Van Der Graaf Generator, which came to nothing.

In November 1974, I auditioned for none other than Love Affair in a garage on a council estate in Hayes, Middlesex, which also came to nothing.

In Summer 1976, I did a lot of auditions, after coming

back from a an ill-fated band venture in Germany called Gypsy Love (with my old mate 'Pierre' Sturgeon). One was with the Edgar Broughton band, who were in the early seventies regarded as a "people's band" who played at all the hippie festivals. They had recorded an album and I had to lay guitar tracks over it. I know that there were lots and lots of other guitarists going for this gig, and once again, nothing ever came of it.

It might sound like that I am a failed auditioner, but there were lots of bands that I did get the job with and one of them in January '76 was Snatch (which included my old mate Danny Hynes, who I was later with in Weapon). I was up against Steve Forrest, previously in Silverhead, a band I had seen in summer '74 at the London Roundhouse and particularly liked. We were both playing together, 'battling it out' as it were, and much to my surprise and delight, I got the gig!

Over the past few years, my playing in bands has somewhat slowed down. I run the occasional jam session and have performed in various bands, currently playing, although sporadically, with Firebird Seven, which is a blues combo, including keyboards and sax. The sax player at one time, was none other than John Guest, who has in his chequered past, played with Wilson Pickett, David Essex, Alvin Stardust and Tommy Steele and countless others!

If it wasn't for Hank Marvin, Duane Eddy and Bert Weedon, I wouldn't have been writing this book now...

I have had some amazing adventures... and some pretty damn hairy moments, but it's all in the name of rock 'n' roll, and I ask for fifty-nine other offences to be taken into consideration!

BOB SAWYER: IRON MAIDEN

SNATCH: Jan - April '76

Me	Danny Hynes	Baz Downes	Darryl Read
(gtr)	(vocals)	(bass/vocals)	(drums) — Died 2013

SHADY LADY: Aug - Nov '76

Me rep Dave Coldwell	Jamie Crompton	Terri Julians
(gtr)	(drums)	(vocals)

Samson
Bad Company   New Hearts
Humble Pie   Suzi Quatro
       Wishbone Ash

IRON MAIDEN #2 Dec '76 - July '77

Me	Dave Murray	Steve Harris	Dennis Willcock	Ron Rebel
(gtr)	(gtr)	(bass)	(voc)	(drums)
			V1	Thunderstick/Torme McCoy
			Gibraltar	Samson

PRAYING MANTIS #2 Jan - July '80

Me	Tino Troy	Chris Troy	Dave Potts rep Mick Ransome
(gtr/voc)	(gtr/voc)	(bass/voc)	(drums)

WEAPON #2: July - Nov '81

Me	Danny Hynes	Baz Downes	Bruce Bisland	Jeff Summers
(gtr)	(vocals)	(bass/vocals)	(drums)	(gtr/vocals)
	Paddy Goes To Holyhead		Sweet	Wildfire
				State Trooper

NITRO BLUES: Late '85 - 2003 (official break)

Me	Foster	John Kitch	Various Others
(gtr/voc)	(bass/growling)	(drums)	(harmonica etc)

BLOODLESS COUP: 2007-2012

Me	Dr' John Guest	Jai Hobbs	Paul Francis	Jevon 'Bear' Ellis	Ron Leek
(gtr/voc)	(sax)	(harp/voc)	(drums)	(keys)	(bass)

FIREBIRD SEVEN: 2012-?

Me	Keith Burnham rep Pete Jenkins	Kev Riddles	Dave Gaskell	Jevon 'Bear' Ellis
(gtr/voc)	(sax)	(bass)	(drums/voc)	(keys)

DR'JOHN GUEST: Previously from... SHANE FENTON, WILSON PICKETT, DAVID ESSEX, TOMMY STEELE!
DAVE POTTS: Previously from... MANDRAKE PADDLE STEAMERS, SKIP BIFFERTY, CRYIN' SHAMES, ALVIN LEE
KEV RIDDLES: Previously from... ANGELWITCH, TYTAN
DARRYL REED: Previously from... RAY MANZAREK (EX-DOORS!)
BAZ DOWNES: Previously from... INNER CITY UNIT (EX-HAWKWIND)

I also played in: BIG LADDER WOMAN '72-'73; MOBY DICK '74; STONE KERB '74-'75; NITRO '75; SLOW MOTION '78; XERO Oct '79; HIGH ROLLER '82-'85; EARTHSIGN 2003-2007. And this is the simplified version. ©Bob 'Angelo' Sawyer 2015

ACKNOWLEDGEMENTS

And for those who do deserve credit... I would like to thank firstly, my wife Melinda for sticking with a twat like me through thick and thin and for the many (and I do mean many) hours she has spent typing this book, whilst trying to decipher my child-like handwriting. I will love you forever.

My old mate (and guitarist with Tank) Cliff Evans who introduced me to Steve Goldby (of MetalTalk) who in turn, introduced me to Jerry and Gary at Wymer Publishing and also to my mate and rock trivia fanatic Stu Tovell for his support in those dark, early days of writing this book. See you all in the next world... 'an don't be late!

To the best of my knowledge and belief, everything contained in this book is factual and without prejudice.